AT WAR
WITH WAR

SEYMOUR CHWAST

AT WAR WITH WAR

5000 Years
of Conquests,
Invasions,
and Terrorist
Attacks

An Illustrated
Timeline

SEVEN STORIES PRESS

New York
Oakland
London

For Pam, Eve and Paula

Copyright © 2017 by Seymour Chwast
Introduction © 2017 by Victor Navasky
Art and design by Seymour Chwast
Camille Murphy, associate designer

A PUSHPIN EDITIONS BOOK
Steven Heller/Seymour Chwast

SEVEN STORIES PRESS
140 Watts Street
New York, NY 10013
www.sevenstories.com

College professors may order examination copies
of Seven Stories Press titles for free.
To order, visit www.sevenstories.com/textbook
or send a fax on school letterhead to (212) 226-1411.

LIBRARY OF CONGRESS CATALOGING-IN-PUBLICATION DATA
Names: Chwast, Seymour, cartoonist. | Container of (expression):
    Sunzi, active 6th century B.C. Sunzi bing fa. English. | Container
    of (expression): Erasmus, Desiderius, −1536 Querela pacis. English. |
    Container of (expression): Bourne, Randolph Silliman, 1886−1918.
    War is the health of the state.
Title: At war with war / Seymour Chwast.
Description: New York : Seven Stories Press, 2017.
Identifiers: LCCN 2017001833 (print) | LCCN 2017010733 (ebook) |
    ISBN 9781609807795 (pbk.) | ISBN 9781609807801 (E-book)
Subjects: LCSH: War—Philosophy—Comic books, strips, etc. |
    Military art and science—Comic books, strips, etc. | BISAC: COMICS
    & GRAPHIC NOVELS / Nonfiction. | HISTORY / Military / General. |
    HISTORY / World.
Classification: LCC U21.2 .A7375 2017 (print) | LCC U21.2 (ebook) |
    DDC 355.0201—dc23
LC record available at https://lccn.loc.gov/2017001833

Printed in China.

—
9 8 7 6 5 4 3 2 1

Contents

Introduction

Victor Navasky

The power of cartoons and caricatures shouldn't be underestimated. For centuries, tyrants have had their perpetrators censored, imprisoned and otherwise inconvenienced. Nevertheless, most people still regard cartoons as trivia, an example of what Sir Ernst Gombrich, the Austrian art historian, has called "the low medium of illustration." But comes now Seymour Chwast, who makes clear in the following pages just how cartoons and illustrations can be deployed to transmit a message that educates and informs, even as it incites; a message qualitatively beyond anything possible by words alone.

Seymour Chwast, co-founder in 1954, with Edward Sorel and Milton Glaser, of the legendary Push Pin Studios, which revolutionized the world of design, is, at age 85, still deploying his art to give peace a chance.

But the award-winning designer/artist/illustrator harbors no illusions that his graphic timeline depicting wars, conquests, invasions and terrorist attacks dating from 3300 BCE, will put an end to war. "What I do hope is to arouse awareness. To expose war's stupidity. In 5000 years we haven't learned anything. We haven't found a way to avoid destruction and killing. That amazes me."

It also has caused him, with the help of Kickstarter, to give birth to this book.

At War With War, is a sequel to his earlier *A Book of Battles*. It mobilizes black-and-white cartoons to reveal the irrelevance, futility, brutality and absurdity of war. For this peace activist, maybe the times they are a-changin', but as Chwast's images illustrate, "the arrows have turned into H-bombs but that's the only change. The idea of war is as it has always been – to kill people."

To make his point, Chwast has gone out of his way not to give us beautiful or "artistic" pictures. Instead, we get stark black-and-white drawings. "I did not want to make this pretty," he says. "War isn't pretty." As his former Push Pin colleague Milton Glaser notes, his black-and-white images are in the anti-war tradition of German expressionists like Käthe Kollwitz, who worked with drawing, etching and woodcuts. The drawings he has chosen need no elaboration. They are self-explanatory. By making the case against the futility of war in visual terms, Chwast has performed an invaluable service.

His images are simple and, as former Push Pin partner Ed Sorel puts it, "tasteful." (And they complement what Milton Glaser has called "the left-brain logic" of Chwast's anti-war activism by speaking in "the right-brain language of creativity.") Says Chwast: "I end it in 2015 with no happy ending. There is no ending. That seems to be the downside to this book."

And yet Chwast's drawings starkly raise the question: can it really be true that there is no end to war? Abraham Lincoln, who understood the power of images (he once called the Civil War cartoonist Thomas Nast "my number one recruiting sergeant"), said, "we must disenthrall ourselves" from the culture of violence and guns, and then "we shall save our country."

Seymour Chwast, activist, artist, warrior against war, is a world-class disenthraller.

O Lord our God, help us to tear their soldiers
to bloody shreds with our shells; help us to cover their
smiling fields with the pale forms of their patriot
dead; help us to drown the thunder of the guns with the
shrieks of their wounded, writhing in pain...
in the spirit of love, of Him Who is the Source of Love,
and Who is ever-faithful refuge and friend of all
that are sore beset and seek His aid with humble and
contrite hearts. Amen.

Excerpt from "The War Prayer"
Mark Twain

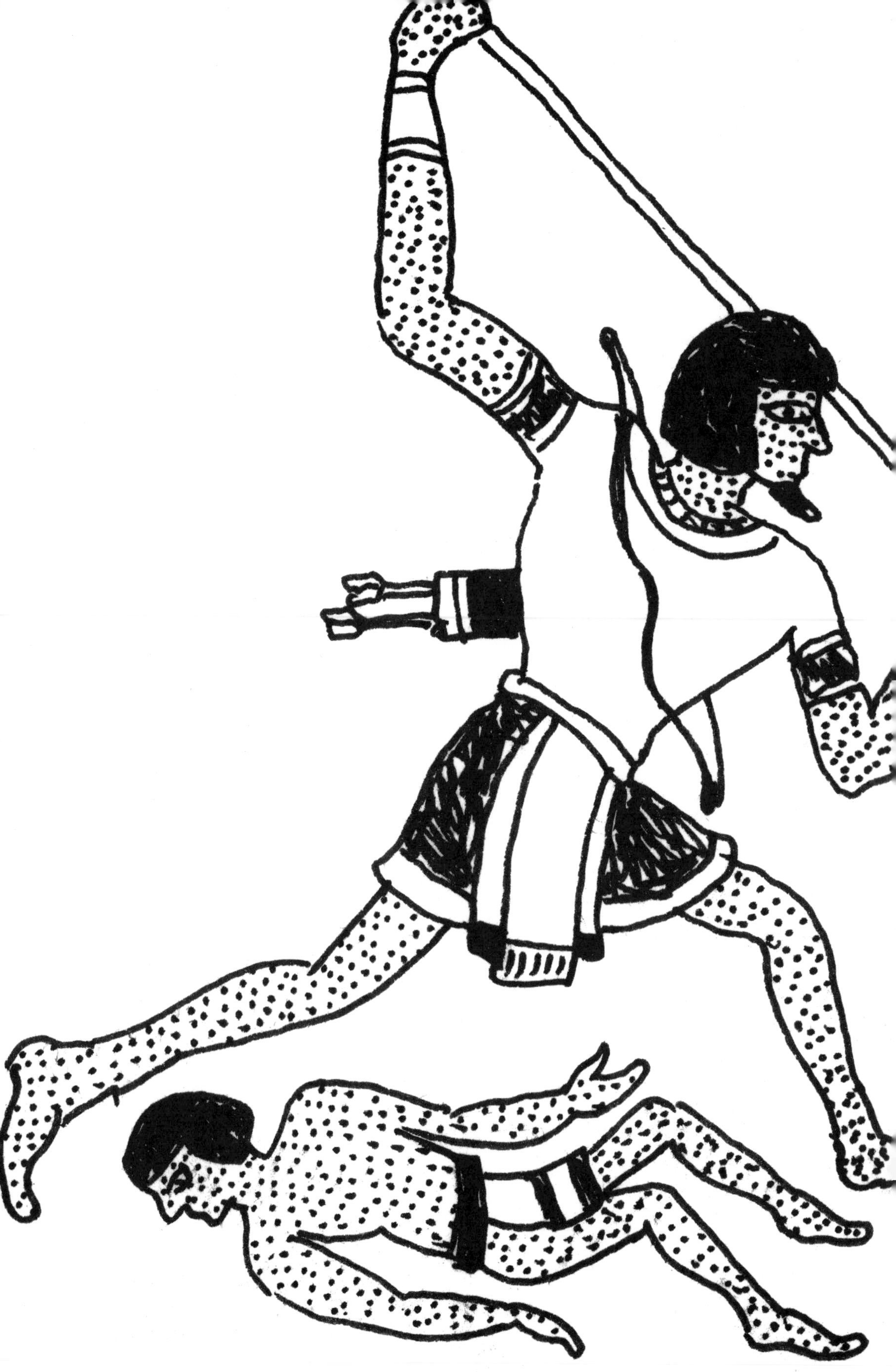

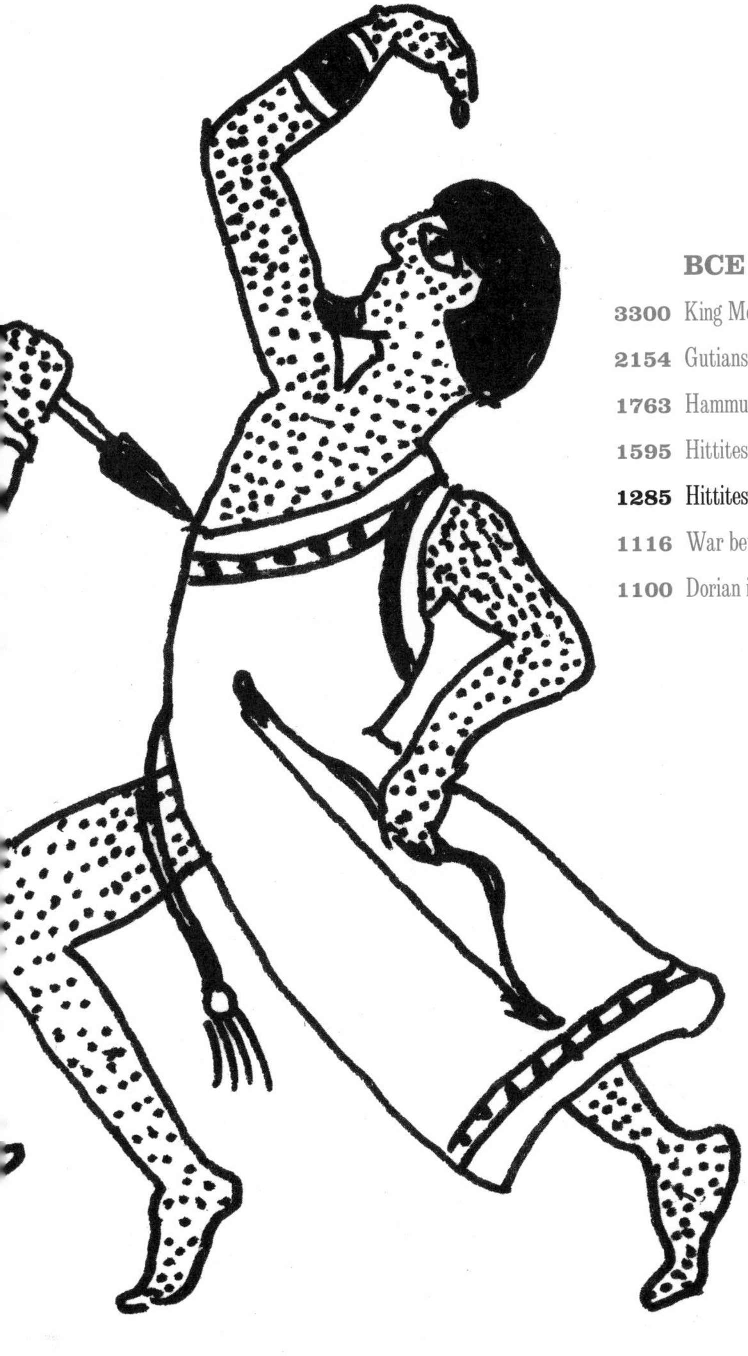

BCE

3300 King Menes, the conqueror, unites Egypt

2154 Gutians overrun southern Mesopotamia

1763 Hammurabi of Babylon conquers Sumer

1595 Hittites sack Babylon

1285 Hittites battle Egyptians at Kadesh

1116 War between Israelites and Philistines

1100 Dorian invasion of southern Greece

945 Libyan prince takes control of the Egyptian delta

745 Tiglath Pileser III conquers Babylon, founds New Assyrian Empire

716 Spartan conquest of Messinia

689 Assyrian king, Sennacherib, conquers Babylon and Judah, threatens Jerusalem

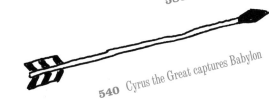

669 Assyrian king, Esarhaddon, conquers northern Egypt

612 Medes and Chaldeans destroy Ninevah

586 Nebuchadnezzar destroys Jerusalem

540 Cyrus the Great captures Babylon

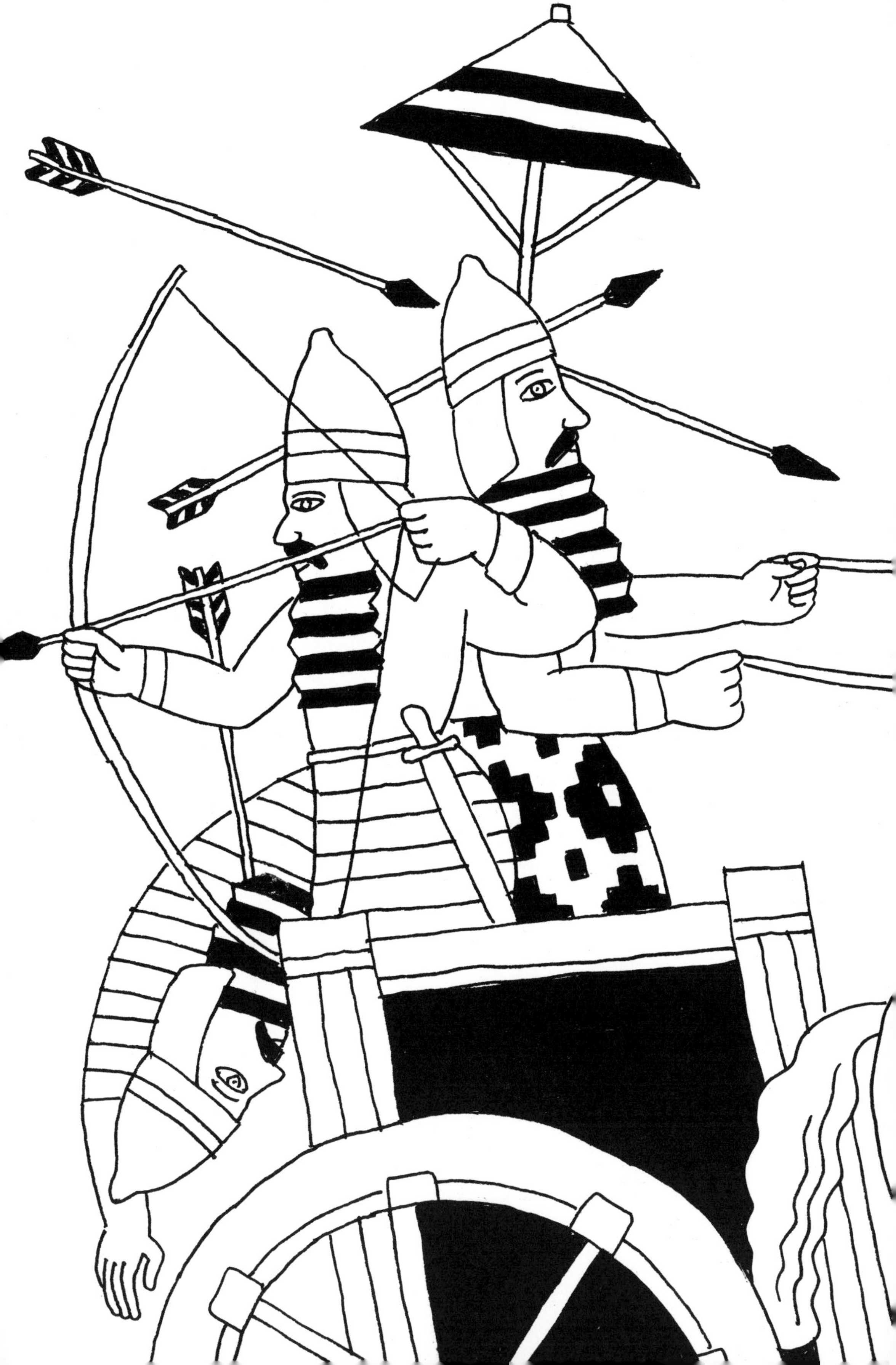

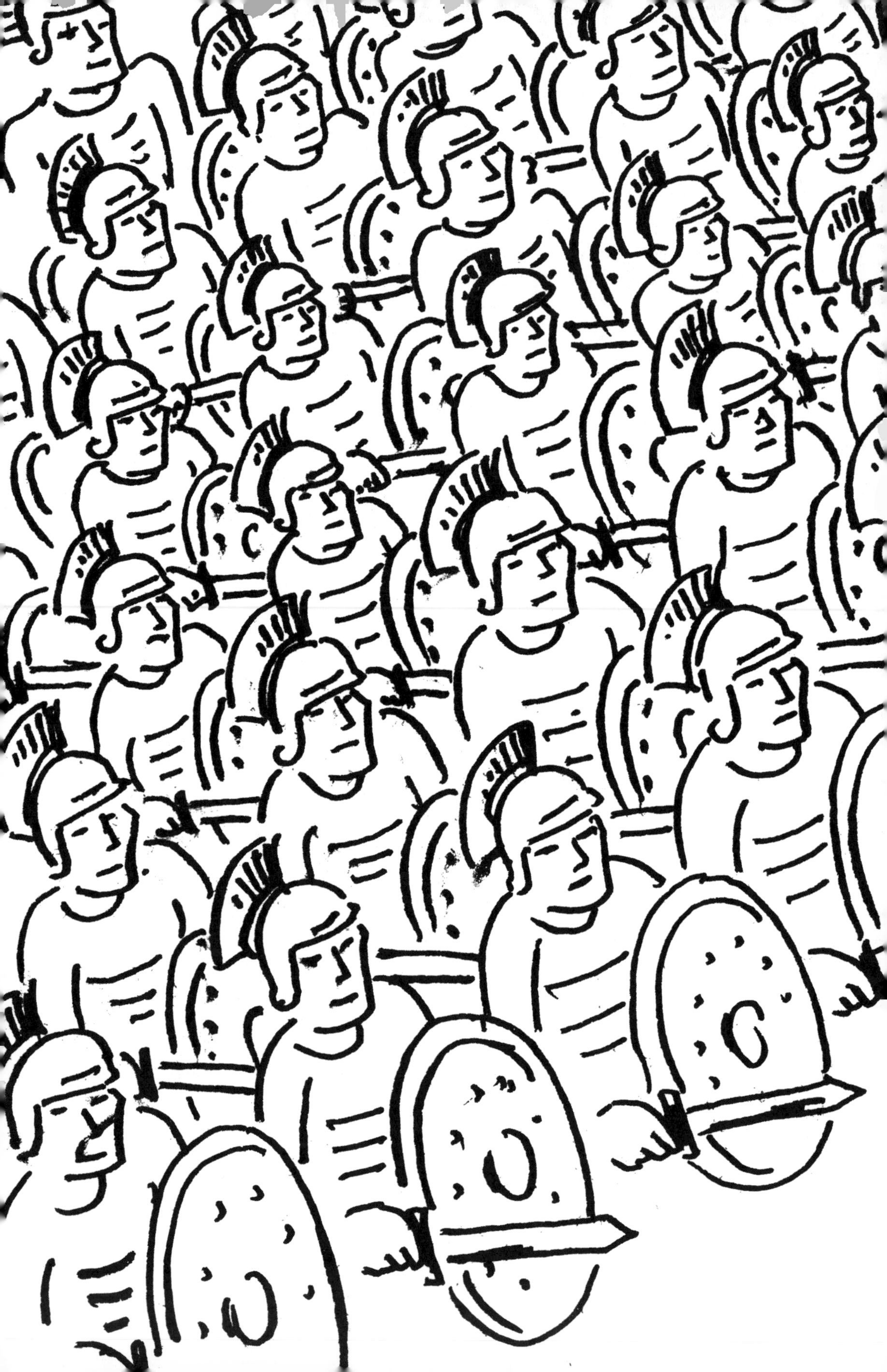

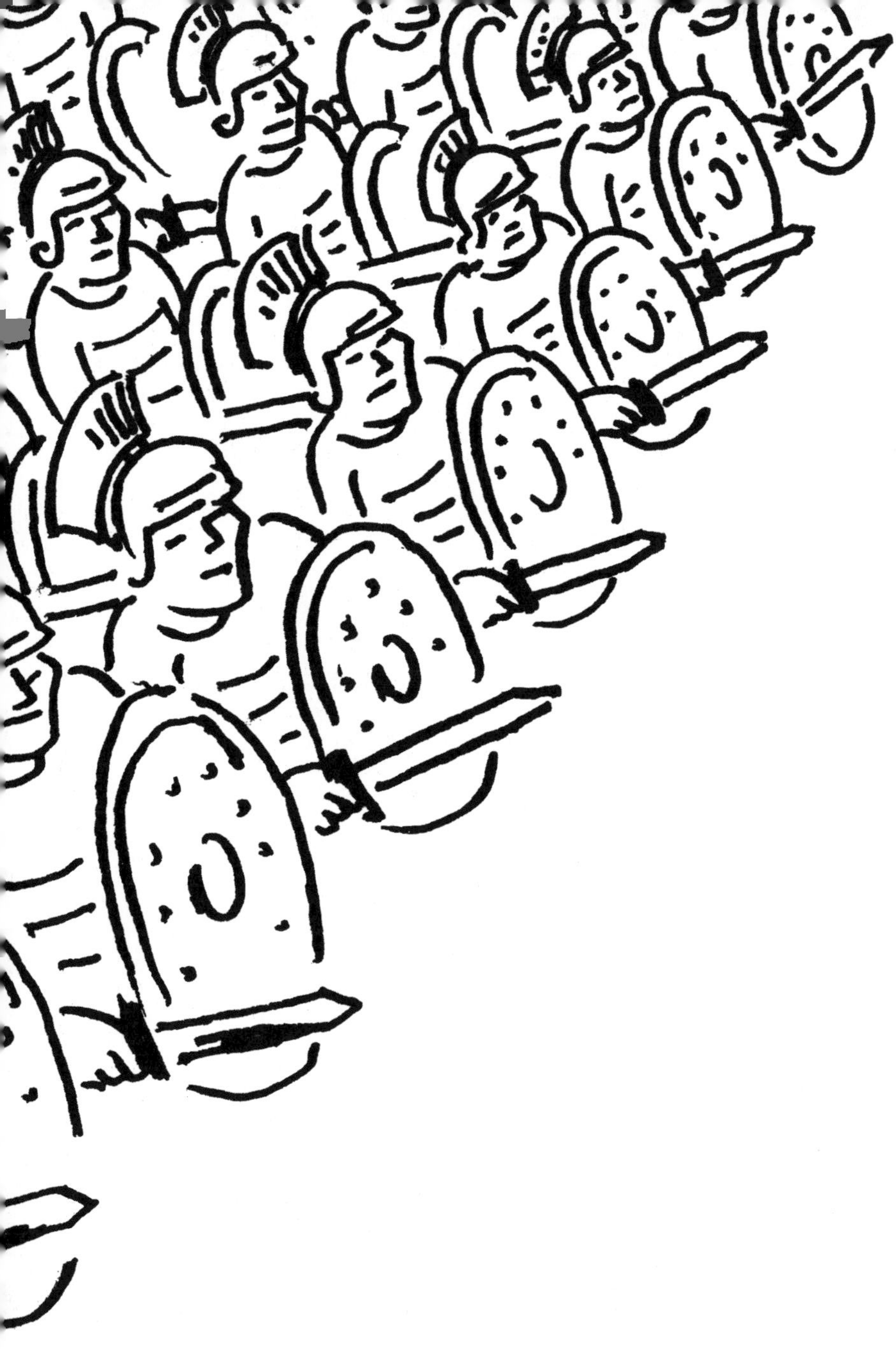

525 Cambyses II of Persia conquers Egypt

496 Battle of Lake Regillus; Rome defeats Latins

490 Greeks defeat Persia at Marathon

480 Xerxes invades Greece

431 **Peloponnesian War between Athens and Sparta begins**

396 Rome captures Etruscan city of Veii

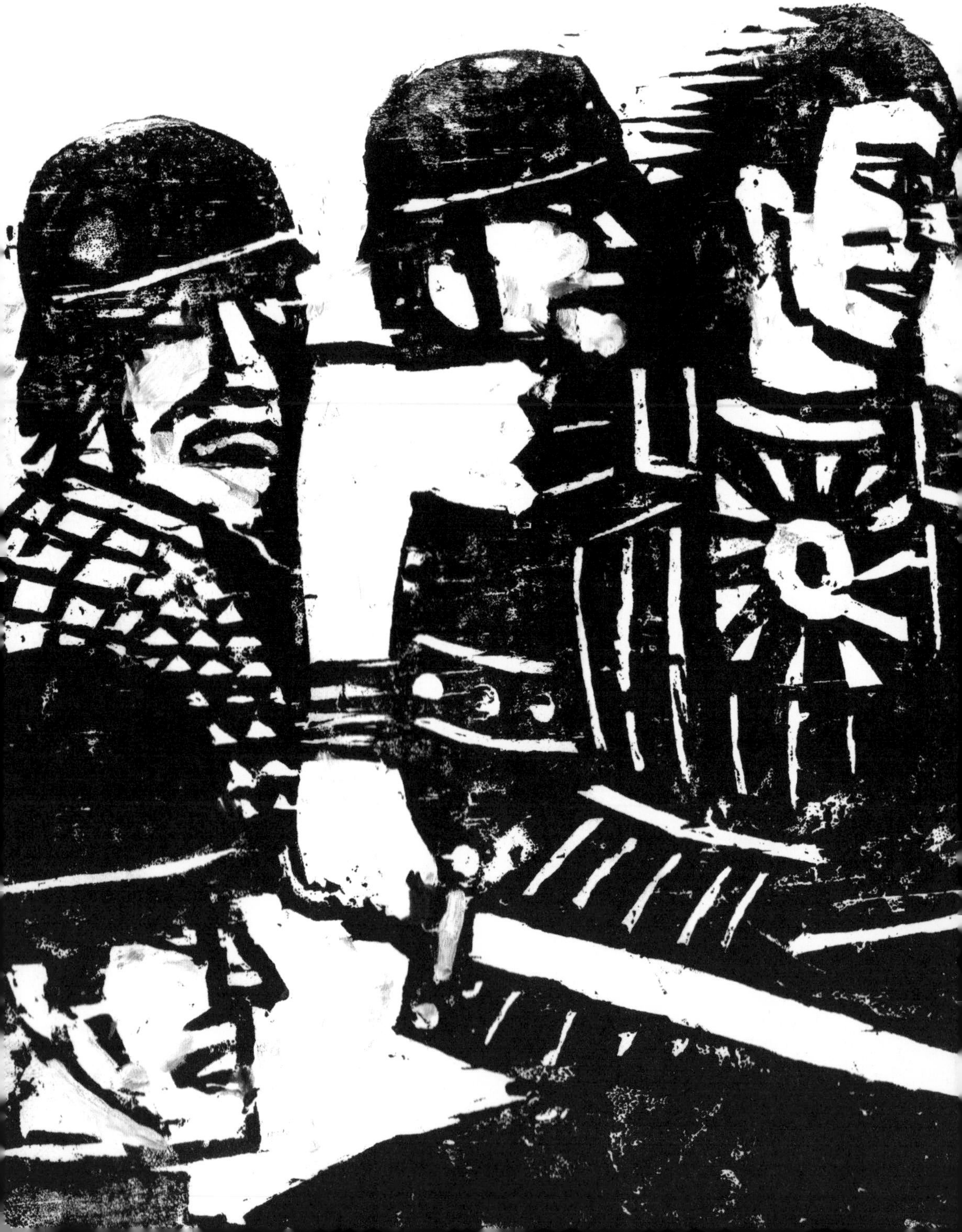

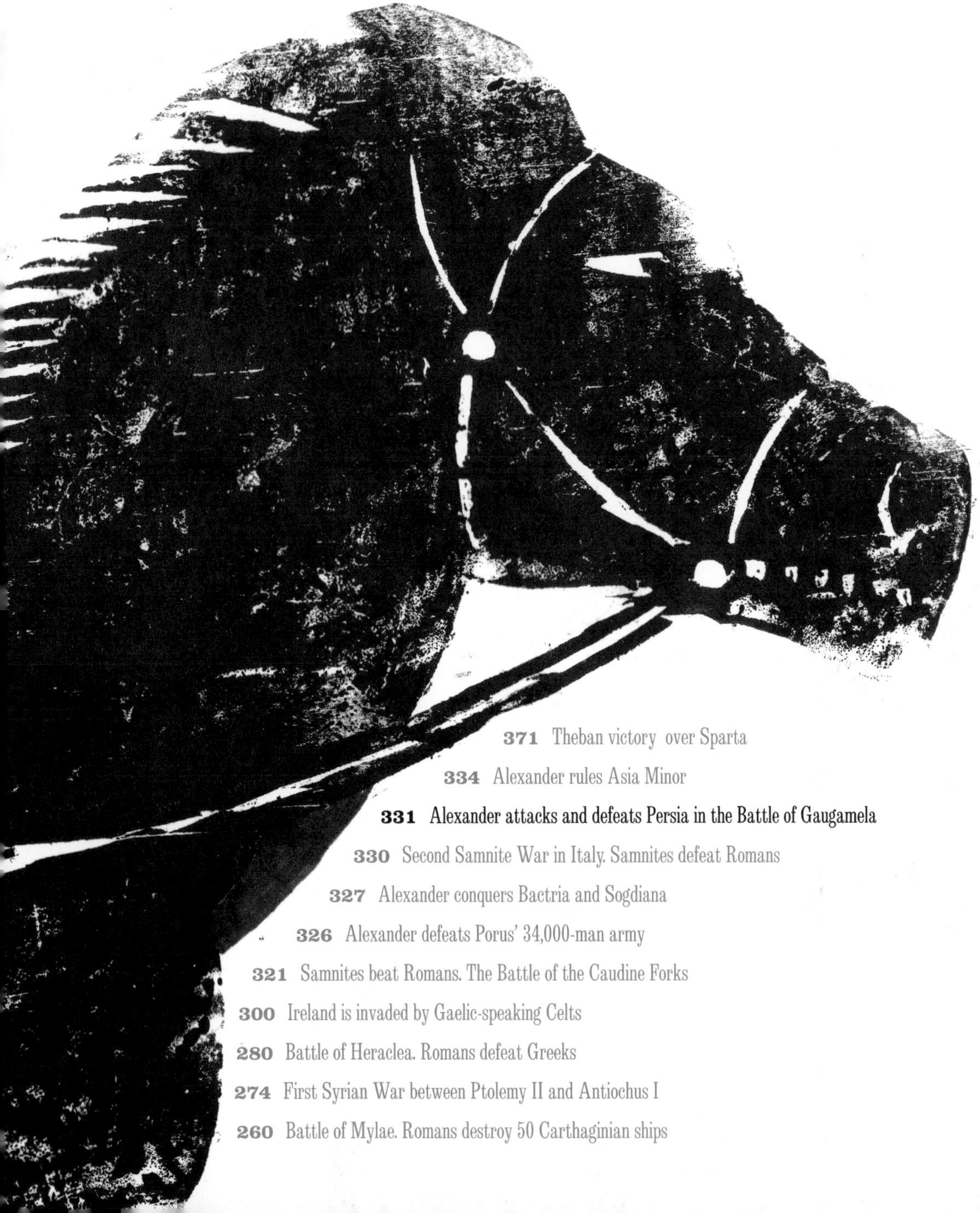

371 Theban victory over Sparta

334 Alexander rules Asia Minor

331 Alexander attacks and defeats Persia in the Battle of Gaugamela

330 Second Samnite War in Italy. Samnites defeat Romans

327 Alexander conquers Bactria and Sogdiana

326 Alexander defeats Porus' 34,000-man army

321 Samnites beat Romans. The Battle of the Caudine Forks

300 Ireland is invaded by Gaelic-speaking Celts

280 Battle of Heraclea. Romans defeat Greeks

274 First Syrian War between Ptolemy II and Antiochus I

260 Battle of Mylae. Romans destroy 50 Carthaginian ships

264 **During the Punic Wars, Rome begins the defeat of Carthage and expansion of the Roman Empire**

255 Roman invasion of northern Africa fails

254 Seleucids and Ptolemies fight a six-year war

225 Roman legions defeat Gallic tribes

205 Ptolemy V loses Judea to Syria

202 Battle of Zama marks the end of the Second Punic War

165 Judas Maccabeus takes Jerusalem

148 Rome is victor in Fourth Macedonian War

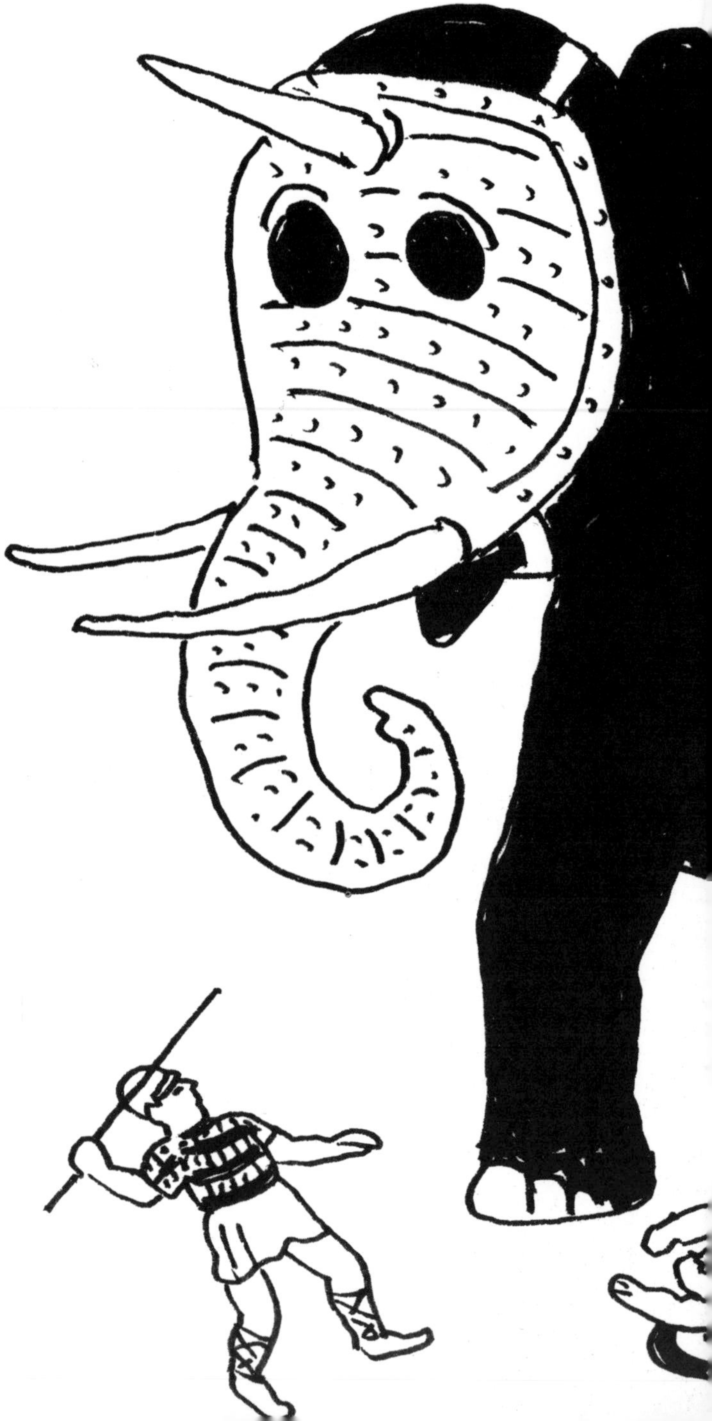

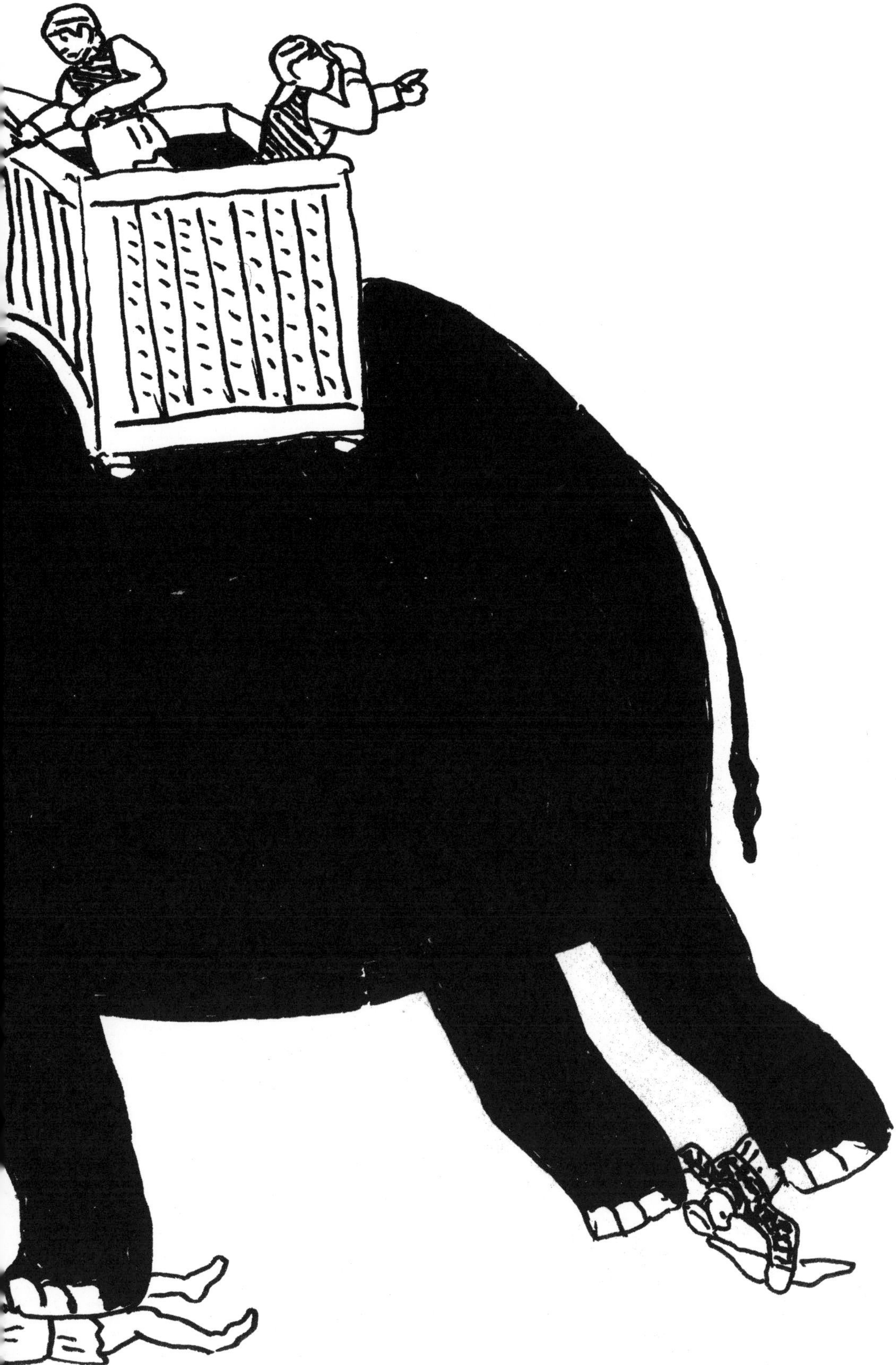

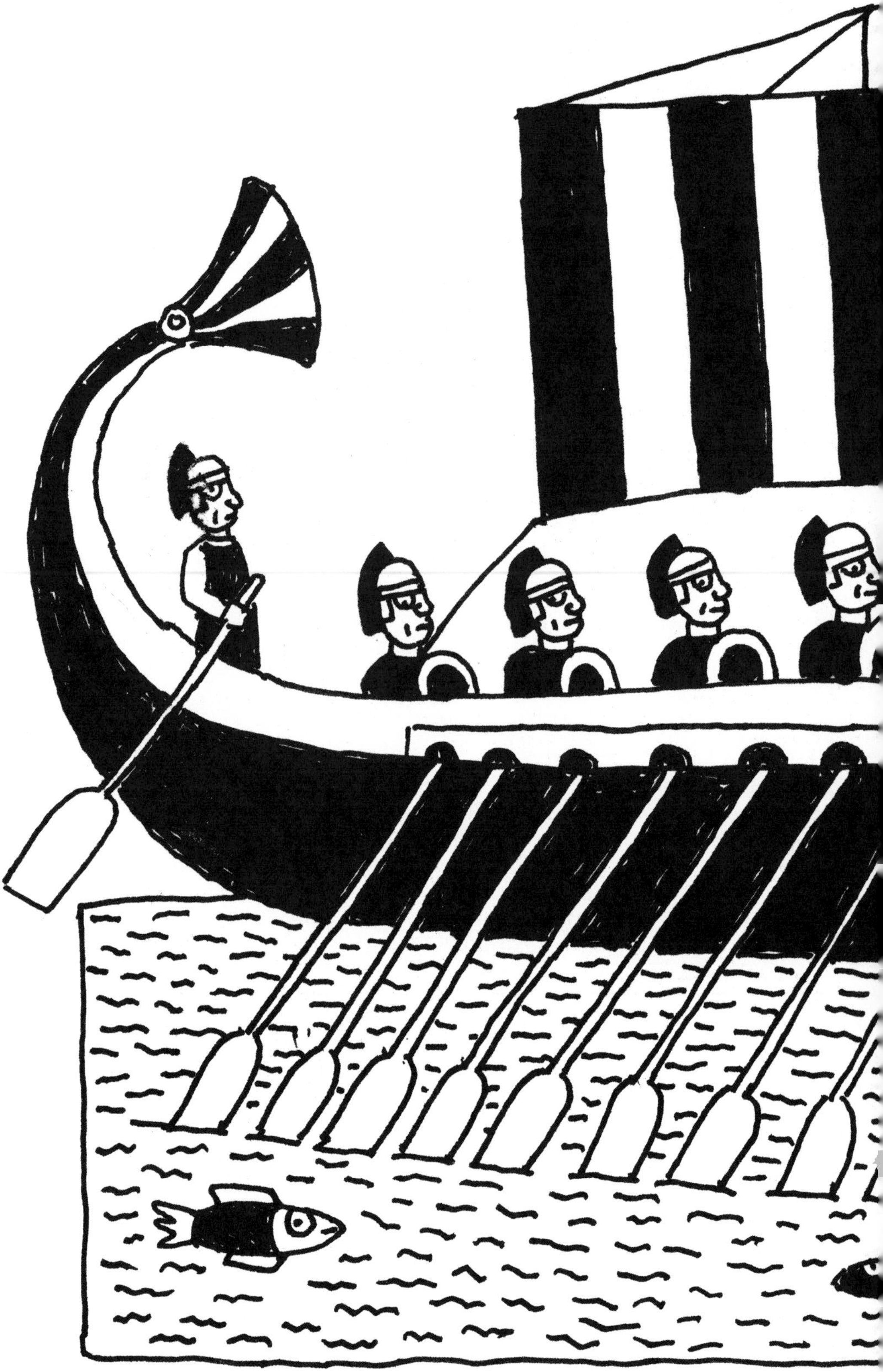

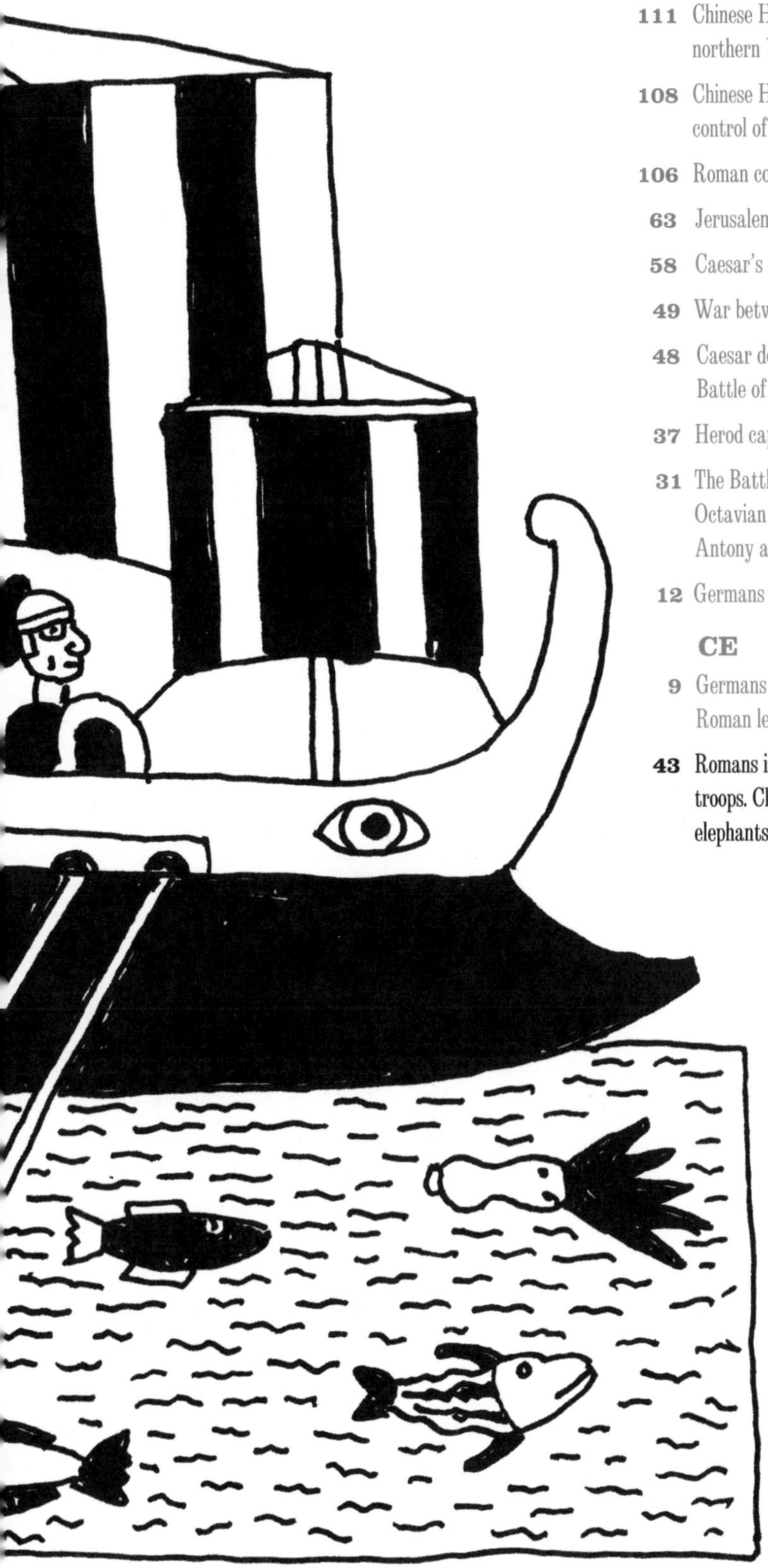

112 Numidia at war with Romans

111 Chinese Han empire conquers northern Vietnam

108 Chinese Han takes military control of the Korean peninsula

106 Roman conquest of Numidia

63 Jerusalem taken by Pompeii

58 Caesar's conquest of Gaul

49 War between Rome and Pompeii

48 Caesar defeats Pompeii at the Battle of Pharsalus, Greece

37 Herod captures Jerusalem

31 The Battle of Actium; Octavian defeats forces of Antony and Cleopatra

12 Germans conquered by Rome

CE

9 Germans destroy three Roman legions

43 Romans invade Britain with 20,000 troops. Claudius arrives with elephants and heavy artillery

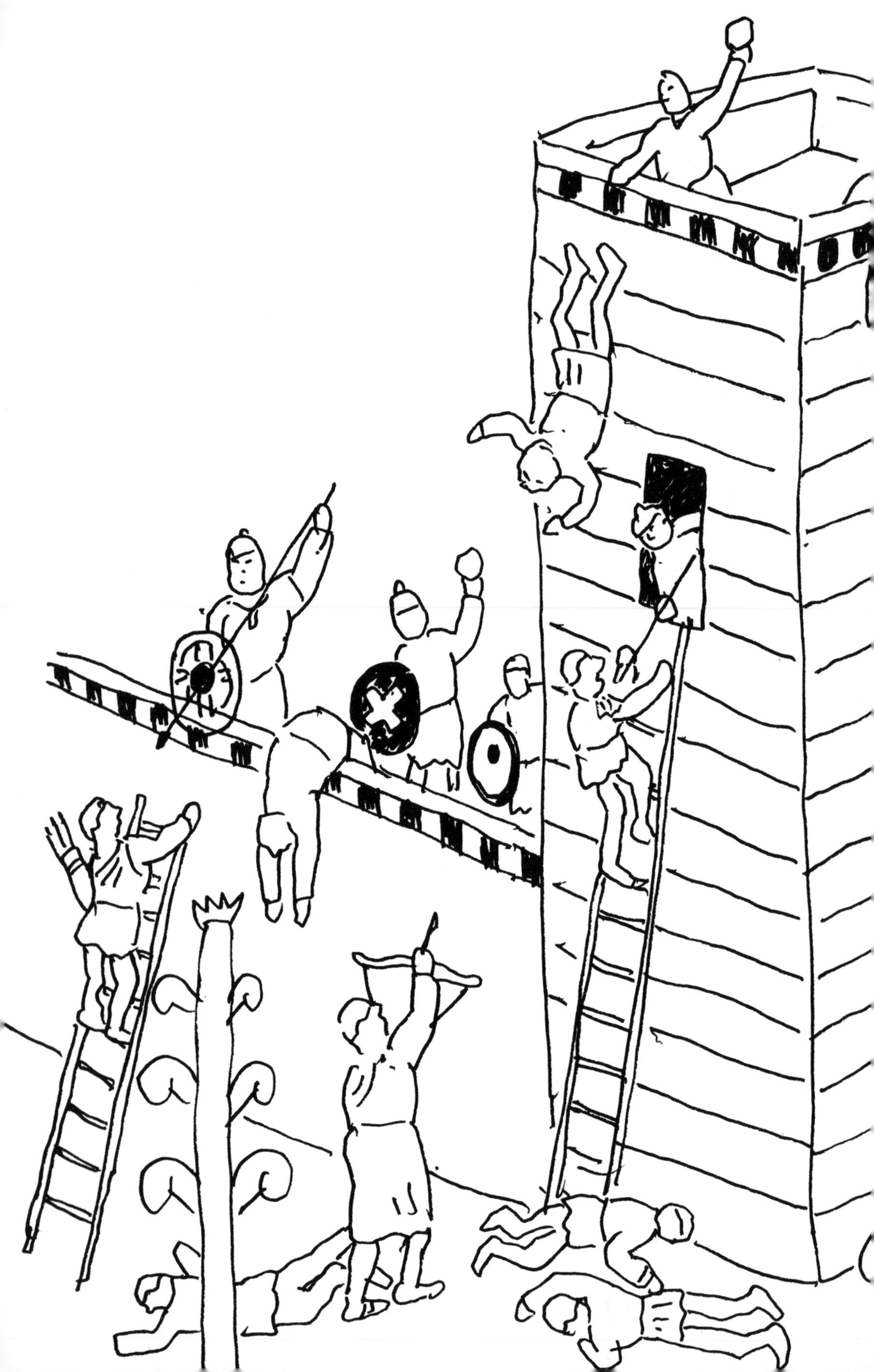

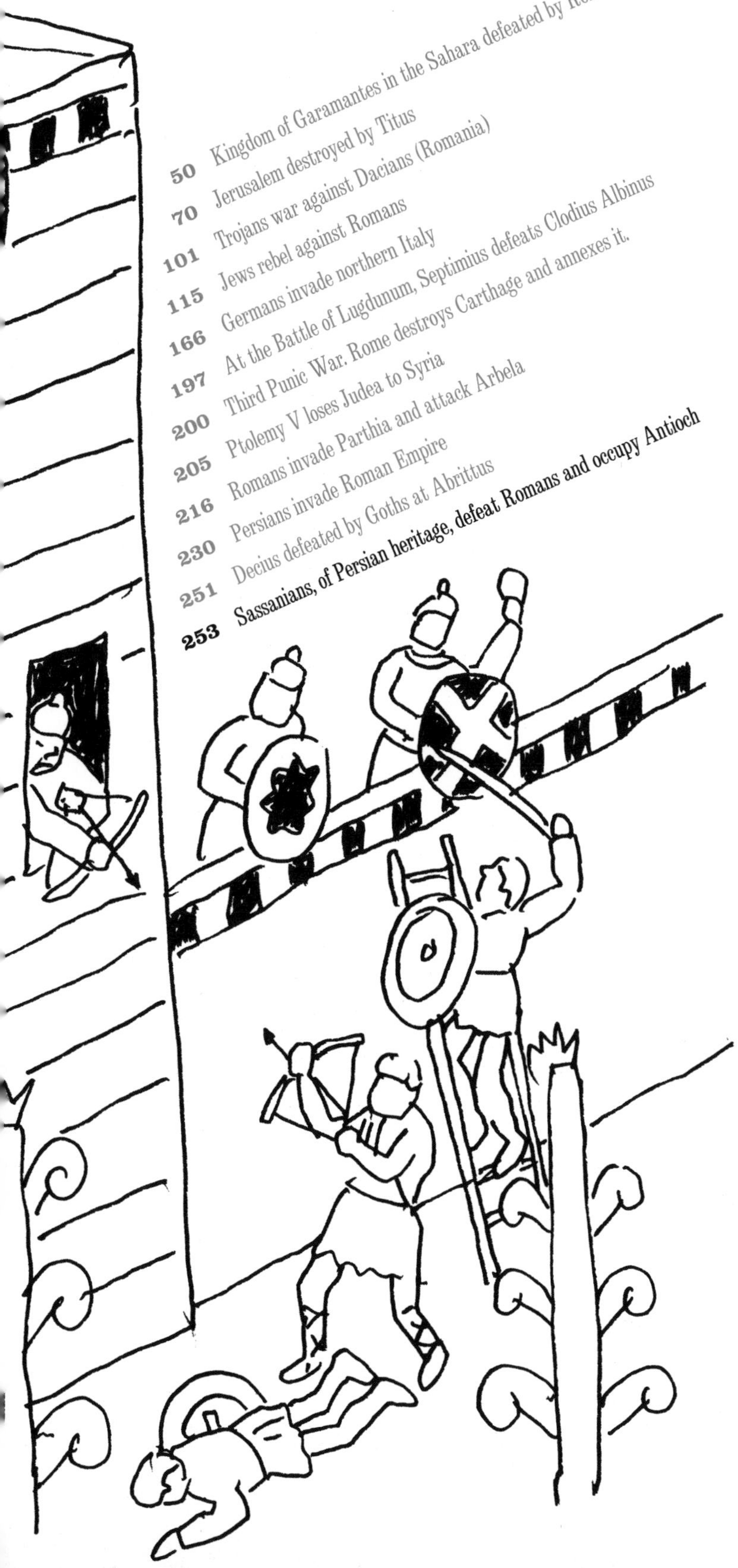

50 Kingdom of Garamantes in the Sahara defeated by Rome

70 Jerusalem destroyed by Titus

101 Trojans war against Dacians (Romania)

115 Jews rebel against Romans

166 Germans invade northern Italy

197 At the Battle of Lugdunum, Septimius defeats Clodius Albinus

200 Third Punic War. Rome destroys Carthage and annexes it.

205 Ptolemy V loses Judea to Syria

216 Romans invade Parthia and attack Arbela

230 Persians invade Roman Empire

251 Decius defeated by Goths at Abrittus

253 Sassanians, of Persian heritage, defeat Romans and occupy Antioch

287 Carausius occupies Britain and northern Gaul

296 Sassanians occupy Armenia and defeat Roman emperor, Galerius

312 Constantine I defeats Maxentius in Battle of Milvian Bridge

348 Battle of Singara. Persians and Romans end fighting in a draw

350 Huns invade Persia and India

360 Persians capture Mesopotamia from Romans

371 Theban victory over Sparta

378 In the Battle of Adrianople, Gothic rebels defeat Romans

393 Japanese invaders capture Silla and Paekche in Korea

401 Alaric, king of the Visigoths, invades Italy

415 Visigoths defeat Siling Vandals

439 Vandals take Carthage

447 Attila the Hun invades Italy but is unable to take Rome. He is unable to take Constantinople as well

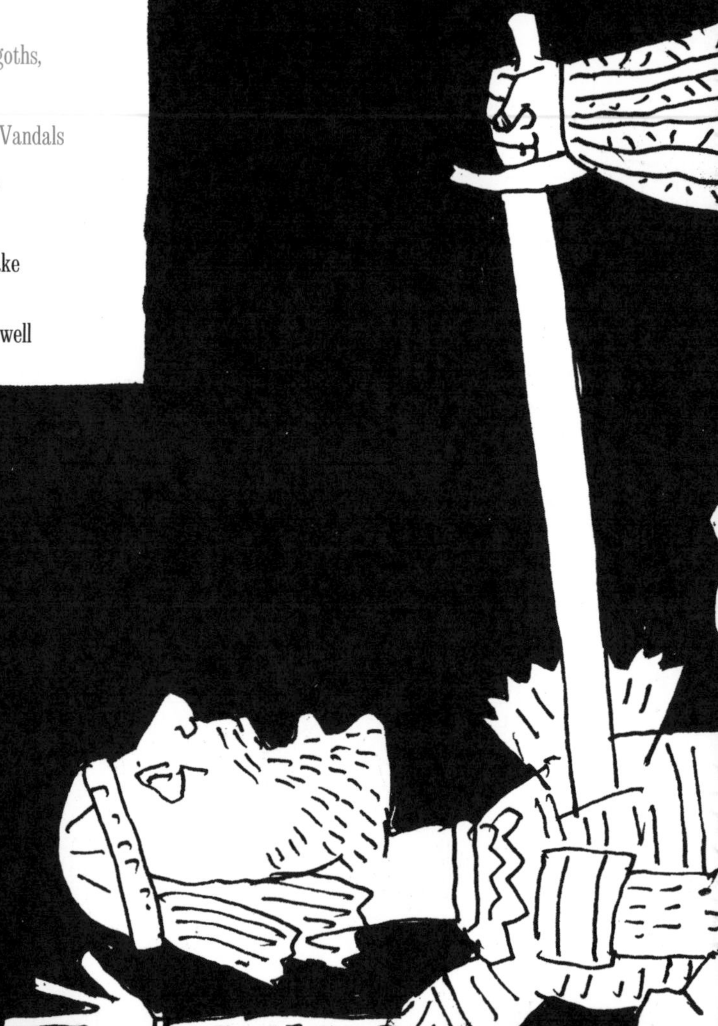

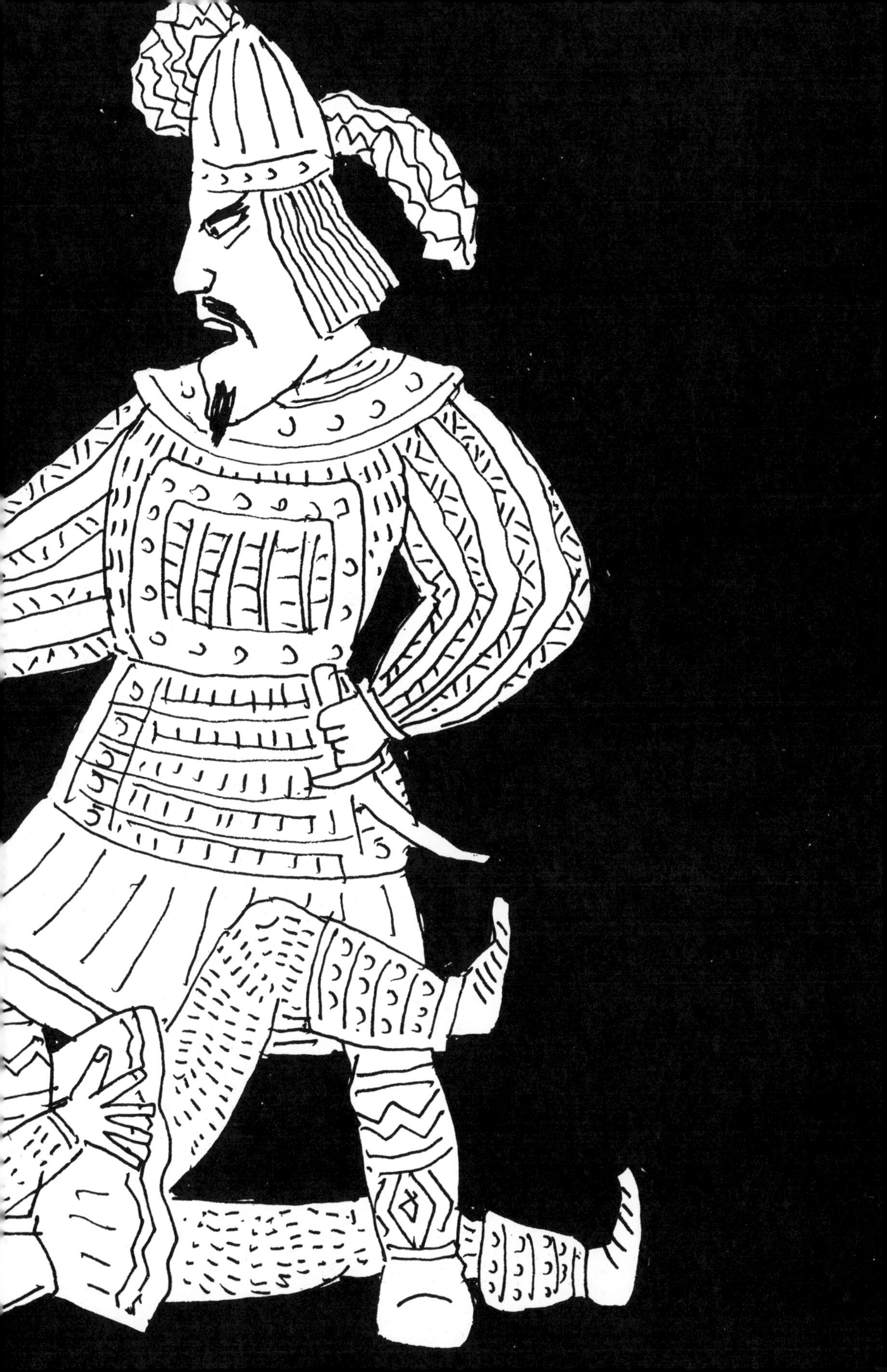

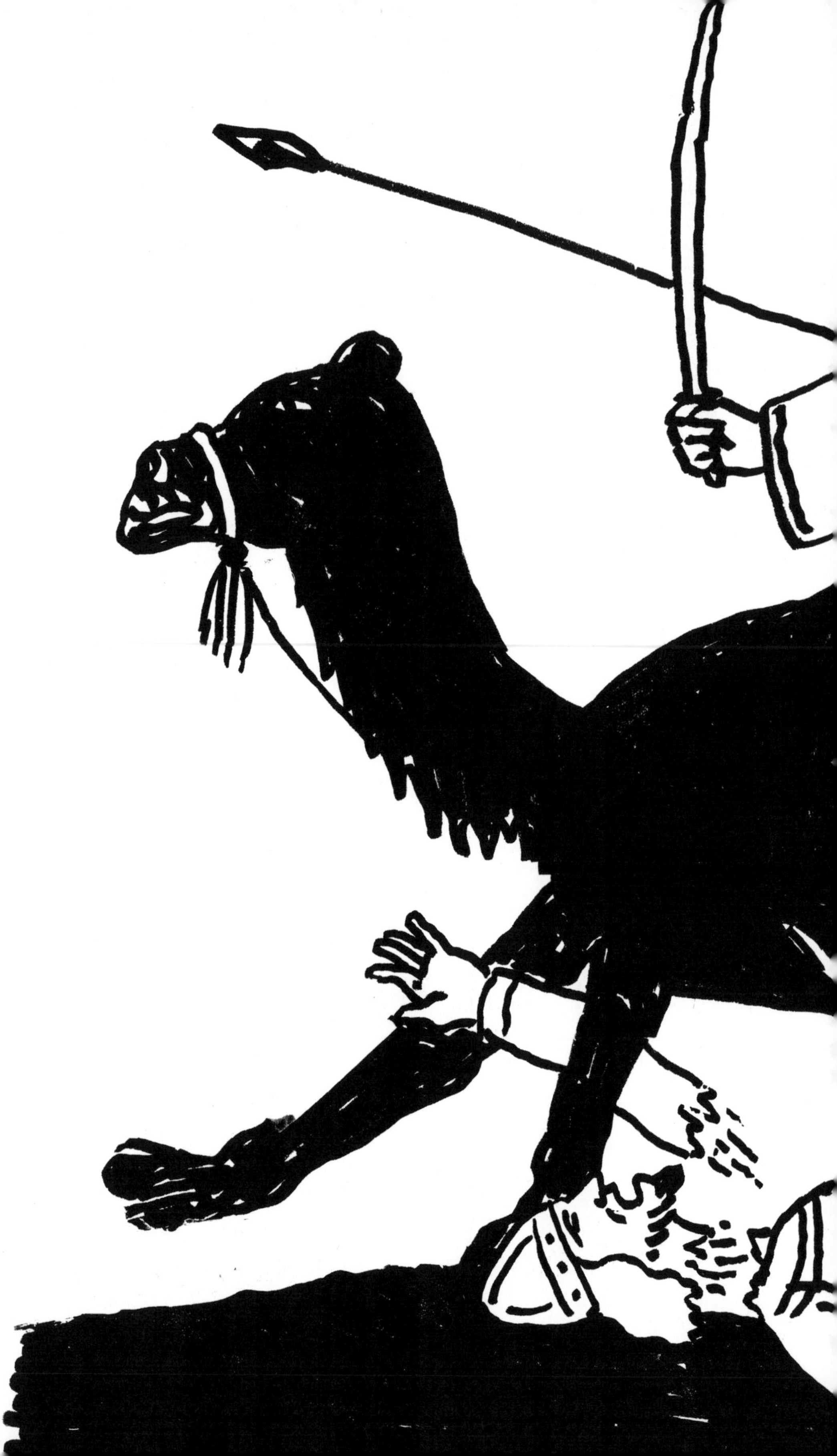

451 In the Battle of Catalaunian Fields, Romans and Goths defeat Attila the Hun

454 Defeat of Athenians in Egypt

455 Vandals, under King Gaiseric, sack Rome

467 Hephthalite Huns capture most of western India

486 Franks conquer Gaul

493 Ostrogoths conquer Italy. Theodoric becomes king

533 Justinian conquers Vandal kingdom in North Africa

535 Byzantines invade southern Italy

614 Persians capture Jerusalem and Asia Minor

628 Byzantines recapture Jerusalem

634 Muslims take Syria in the Battle of Yarmouk

642 Arabs capture Alexandria

650 Khazars conquer Bulgarian empire in southern Russia

663 Byzantine emperor Constantine II invades Italy and sacks Rome

668 Tang forces conquer Koguryo in Korea

711 Arabs invade Spain, defeat Visigoths and Christians

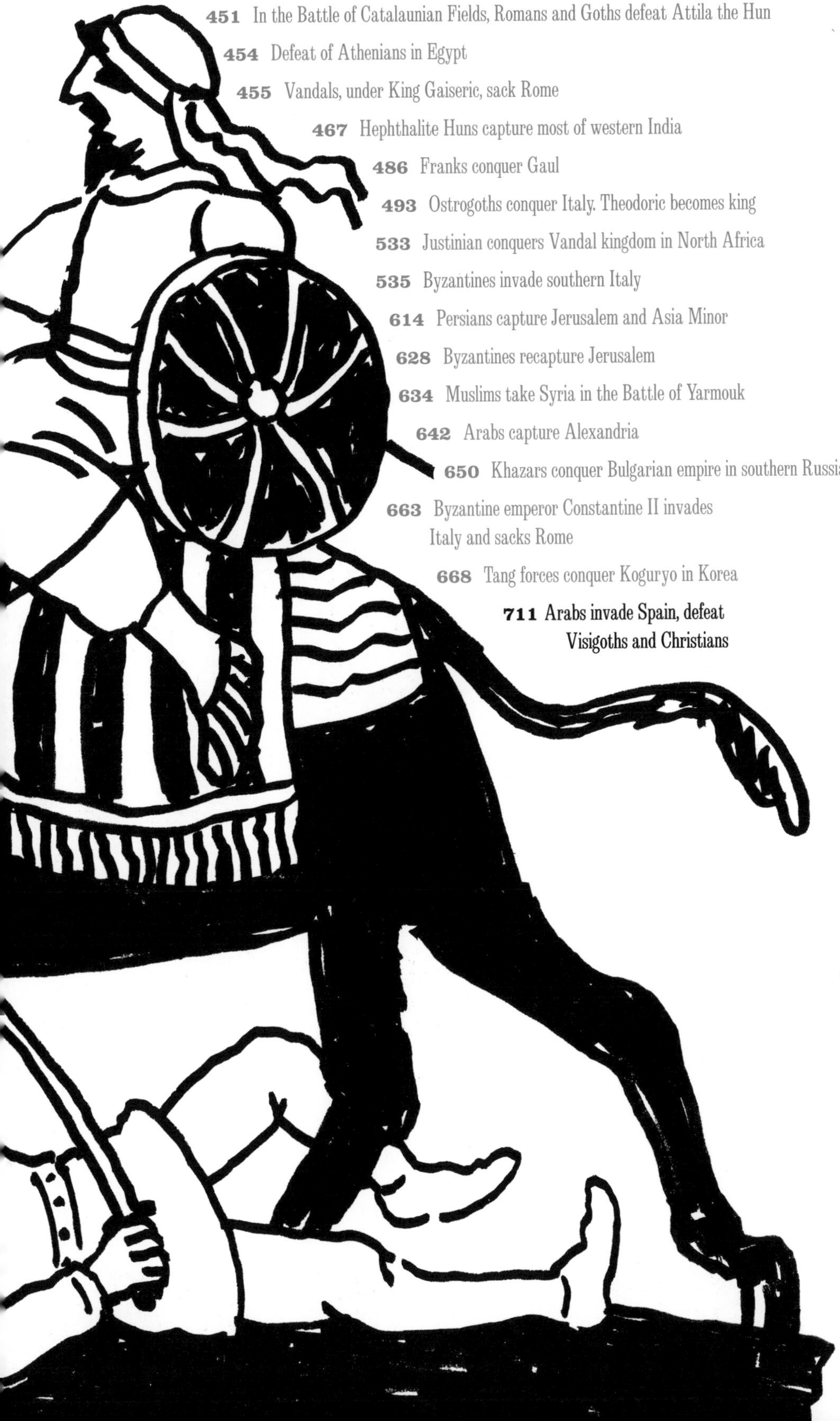

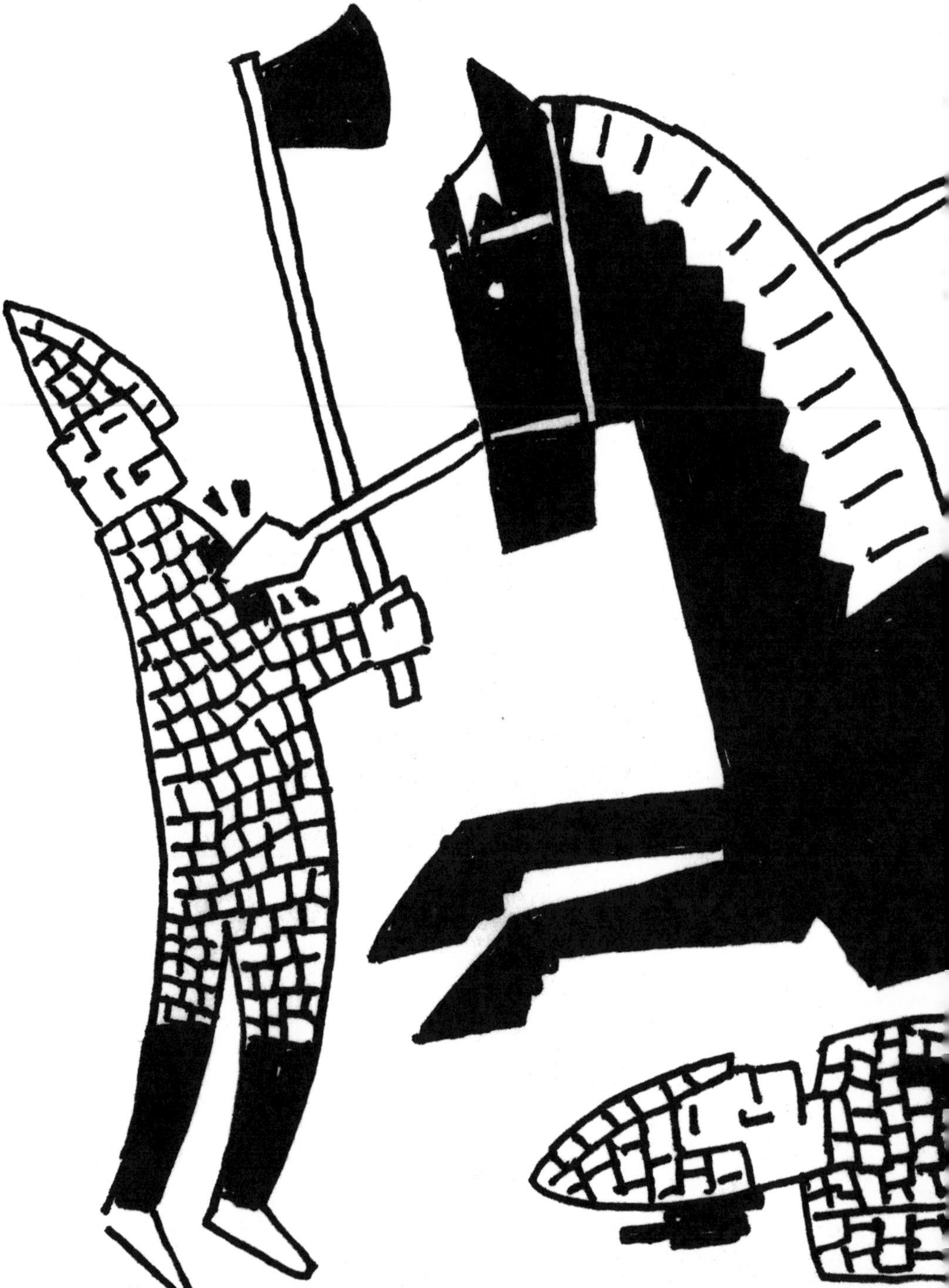

732 Frankish leader, Charles Martel, halts Muslim advance in Battle of Tours
749 Battle of the Zab in Syria. Abbasids control most of the Muslims
778 Byzantines defeat Arabs in the Battle of Germania, Asia Minor
837 Muslims conquer Sicily from Byzantines
885 Saxons recapture London from Vikings
885 Vikings begin siege of Paris
898 Magyars invade Italy and sack Paris
926 Northern Mongols invade northern China, defeat King P'o-Hai
996 Byzantine emperor, Basil II, begins war with Bulgaria
1013 Danish, led by Sweyn I, conquer England
1040 Turks conquer Afghanistan and eastern Persian
1060 Norman invasion of Sicily begins
1063 Seljuk Turks capture Baghdad
1066 **Norman conquest of England with the Battle of Hastings**

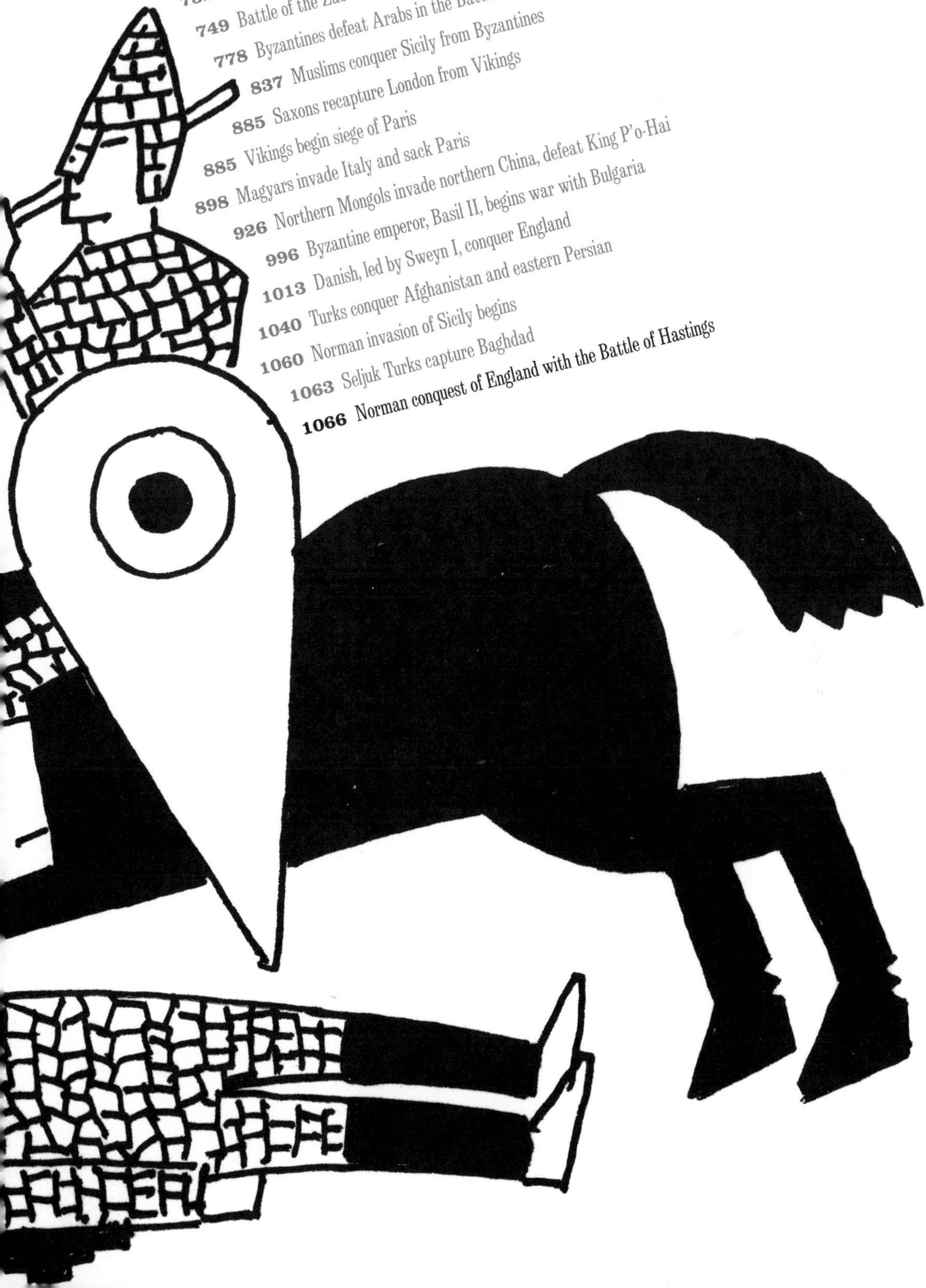

Sun Tzu

The Art of War

This excerpt, from a 2500-year-old treatise, was translated by Lionel Giles.

I. Laying Plans

1 Sun Tzu said: The art of war is of vital importance to the State.

2. It is a matter of life and death, a road either to safety or to ruin. Hence it is a subject of inquiry which can on no account be neglected.

3. The art of war, then, is governed by five constant factors, to be taken into account in one's deliberations, when seeking to determine the conditions obtaining in the field.

4. These are: (1) The Moral Law; (2) Heaven; (3) Earth; (4) The Commander; (5) Method and Discipline.

5, 6. The Moral Law causes the people to be in complete accord with their ruler, so that they will follow him regardless of their lives, undismayed by any danger.

7. Heaven signifies night and day, cold and heat, times and seasons.

8. Earth comprises distances, great and small; danger and security; open ground and narrow passes; the chances of life and death.

9. The Commander stands for the virtues of wisdom, sincerity, benevolence, courage and strictness.

10. By Method and Discipline are to be understood the marshaling of the army in its proper subdivisions, the graduations of rank among the officers, the maintenance of roads by which supplies may reach the army and the control of military expenditure.

11 These five heads should be familiar to every general: he who knows them will be victorious; he who knows them not will fail.

12. Therefore, in your deliberations, when seeking to determine the military conditions, let them be made the basis of a comparison, in this wise:

13. (1) Which of the two sovereigns is imbued with the Moral Law? (2) Which of the two generals has most ability? (3) With whom lie the advantages derived from Heaven and Earth? (4) On which side is discipline most rigorously enforced? (5) Which army is stronger? (6) On which side are officers and men more highly trained? (7) In which army is there the greater constancy both in reward and punishment?

14. By means of these seven considerations I can forecast victory or defeat.

15. The general that hearkens to my counsel and acts upon it, will conquer: let such a one be retained in command! The general that hearkens not to my counsel nor acts upon it, will suffer defeat: let such a one be dismissed!

16. While heading the profit of my counsel, avail yourself also of any helpful circumstances over and beyond the ordinary rules.

17. According as circumstances are favorable, one should modify one's plans.

18. All warfare is based on deception.

19. Hence, when able to attack, we must seem unable; when using our forces, we must seem inactive; when we are near, we must make the enemy believe we are far away; when far away, we must make him believe we are near.

20. Hold out baits to entice the enemy. Feign disorder, and crush him.

21 If he is secure at all points, be prepared for him. If he is in superior strength, evade him.

22. If your opponent is of choleric temper, seek to irritate him. Pretend to be weak, that he may grow arrogant.

23. If he is taking his ease, give him no rest. If his forces are united, separate them.

24. Attack him where he is unprepared, appear where you are not expected.

25. These military devices, leading to victory, must not be divulged beforehand.

26. Now, the general who wins a battle makes many calculations in his temple ere the battle is fought. The general who loses a battle makes but few calculations beforehand. Thus do many calculations lead to victory, and few calculations to defeat: how much more no calculation at all! It is by attention to this point that I can foresee who is likely to win or lose.

II. Waging War

1 Sun Tzu said: In the operations of war, where there are in the field a thousand swift chariots, as many heavy chariots and a hundred thousand mail-clad soldiers, with provisions enough to carry them a thousand li (333 miles), the expenditure at home and at the front, including entertainment of guests, small items such as glue and paint and sums spent on chariots and armor, will reach the total of a thousand ounces of silver per day. Such is the cost of raising an army of 100,000 men.

2. When you engage in actual fighting, if victory is long in coming, then men's weapons will grow dull and their ardor will be damped. If you lay siege to a town, you will exhaust your strength.

3. Again, if the campaign is protracted, the resources of the State will not be equal to the strain.

4. Now, when your weapons are dulled, your ardor damped, your strength exhausted and your treasure spent, other chieftains will spring up to take advantage of your extremity. Then no man, how-ever wise, will be able to avert the consequences that must ensue.

5. Thus, though we have heard of stupid haste in war, cleverness has never been seen associated with long delays.

6. There is no instance of a country having benefited from prolonged warfare.

7. It is only one who is thoroughly acquainted with the evils of war that can thoroughly understand the profitable way of carrying it on.

8. The skillful soldier does not raise a second levy, neither are his supply-wagons loaded more than twice.

9. Bring war material with you from home, but forage on the enemy. Thus the army will have food enough for its needs.

10. Poverty of the State exchequer causes an army to be main-tained by contributions from a distance. Contributing to maintain an army at a distance causes the people to be impoverished.

11 On the other hand, the proximity of an army causes prices to go up; and high prices cause the people's substance to be drained away.

12. When their substance is drained away, the peasantry will be afflicted by heavy exactions.

13, 14. With this loss of substance and exhaustion of strength, the homes of the people will be stripped bare, and three-tenths of their income will be dissipated; while government expenses for broken chariots, worn-out horses, breast-plates and helmets, bows and arrows, spears and shields, protective mantles, draught-oxen and heavy wagons, will amount to four-tenths of its total revenue.

15. Hence a wise general makes a point of foraging on the enemy. One cartload of the enemy's provisions is equivalent to twenty of one's own, and likewise a single picul of his provender is equivalent to twenty from one's own store.

16. Now in order to kill the enemy, our men must be roused to anger; that there may be advantage from defeating the enemy, they must have their rewards.

17. Therefore in chariot fighting, when ten or more chariots have been taken, those should be rewarded who took the first. Our own flags should be substituted for those of the enemy, and the chariots mingled and used in conjunction with ours. The captured soldiers should be kindly treated and kept.

18. This is called using the conquered foe to augment one's own strength.

19. In war, then, let your great object be victory, not lengthy campaigns.

20. Thus it may be known that the leader of armies is the arbiter of the people's fate, the man on whom it depends whether the nation shall be in peace or in peril.

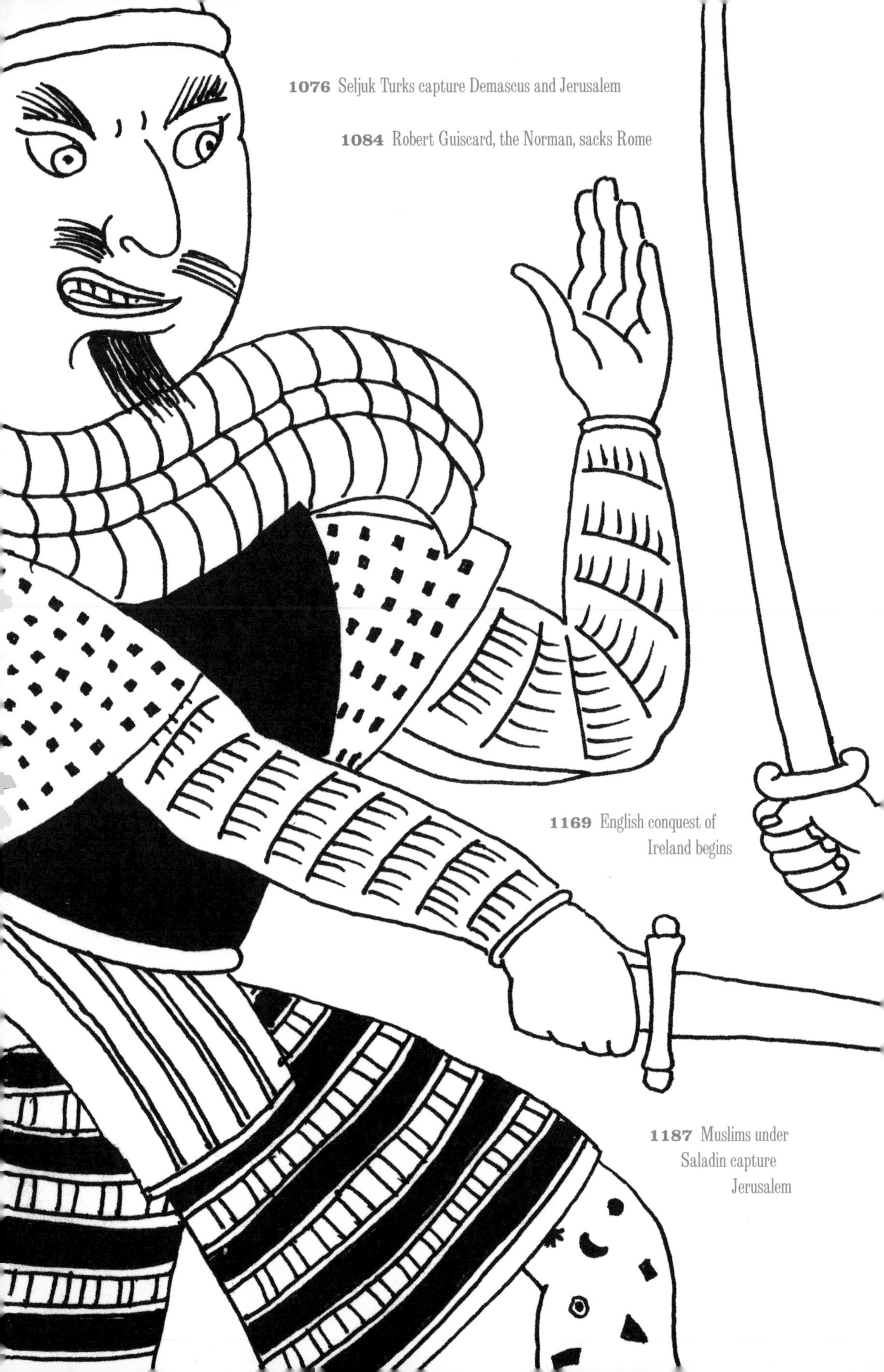

1076 Seljuk Turks capture Demascus and Jerusalem

1084 Robert Guiscard, the Norman, sacks Rome

1169 English conquest of Ireland begins

1187 Muslims under Saladin capture Jerusalem

1096 The First Crusade, an attempt to capture the Holy Lands by Pope Urban II

1099 Crusaders capture Jerusalem

1102 Boleslaw of Poland conquers Pomerania on the southern shore of the Baltic Sea

1109 War between France and England

1138 David I of Scotland invades England

1156 War between two Japanese clans, the Taira and the Minamoto

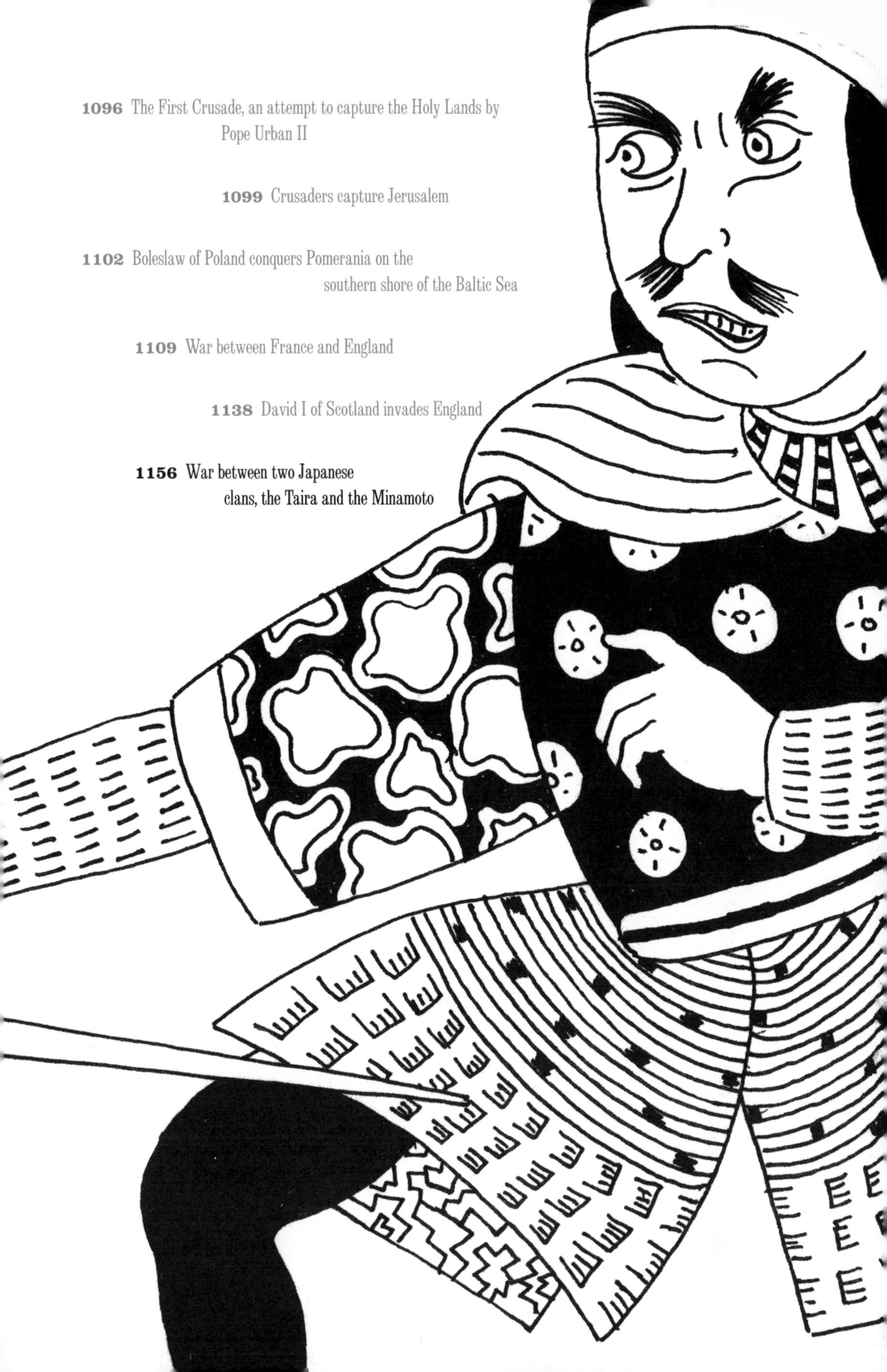

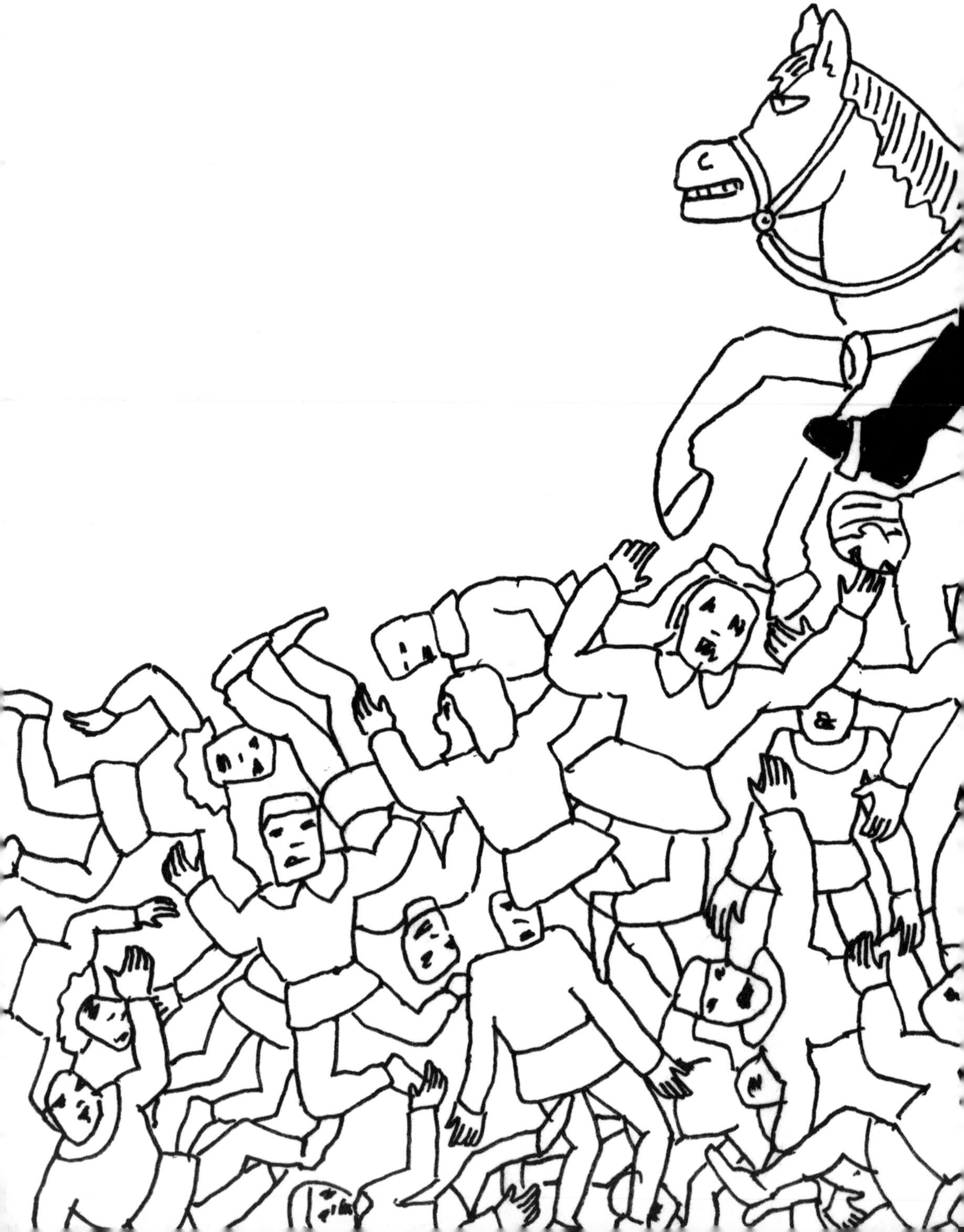

1189 Third Crusade

1191 Richard the Lionheart seizes Cyprus

1202 Fourth Crusaders take Constantinople

1208 Genghis Khan conquers Turkestan

1215 Mongol leader Genghis Khan, creator of the largest empire in the world, conquers Beijing

1218 Genghis Khan conquers Persia

1218 Fifth Crusade

1228 Sixth Crusade

1235 Bulgarians conquer Thrace and attack Constantinople

1241 Mongols invade Poland and Hungary

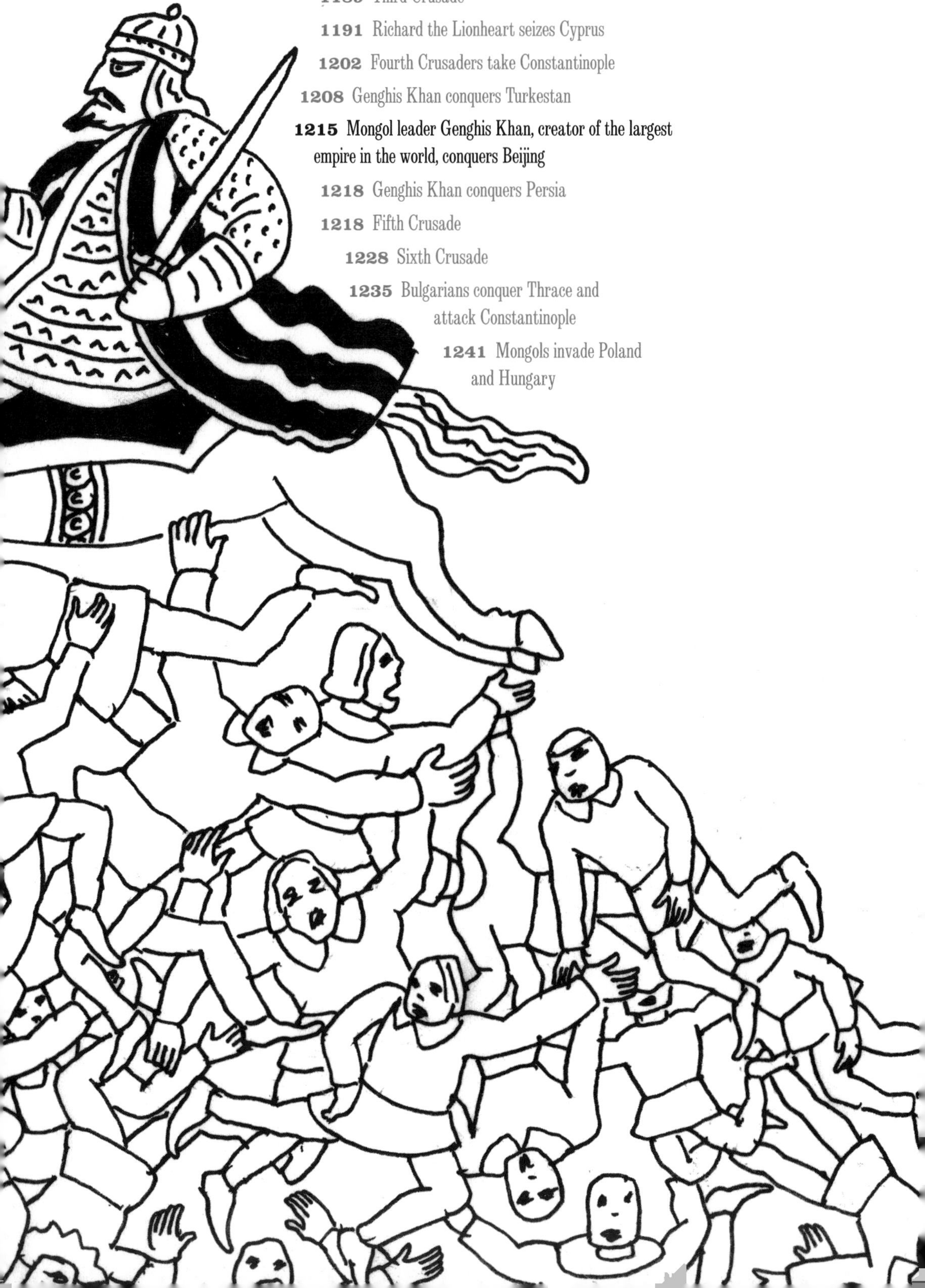

1241 Muslim victory at Liegnitz in Silesia

1249 Sweden conquers Finland

1250 Sultanate Mamluks from the Caucasus take Syria and Egypt

1260 Tuscan Ghibellines defeat Florentine Guelfs at the Battle of Montaperti

1261 Michael III, emperor of Nicaea, restores Byzantine Empire

1270 Eighth Crusade

1280 Mongols conquer Pagan in Burma

1283 **Teutonic knights conquer Prussia after fighting for more than 50 years. Unbaptized Prussians are killed or exiled**

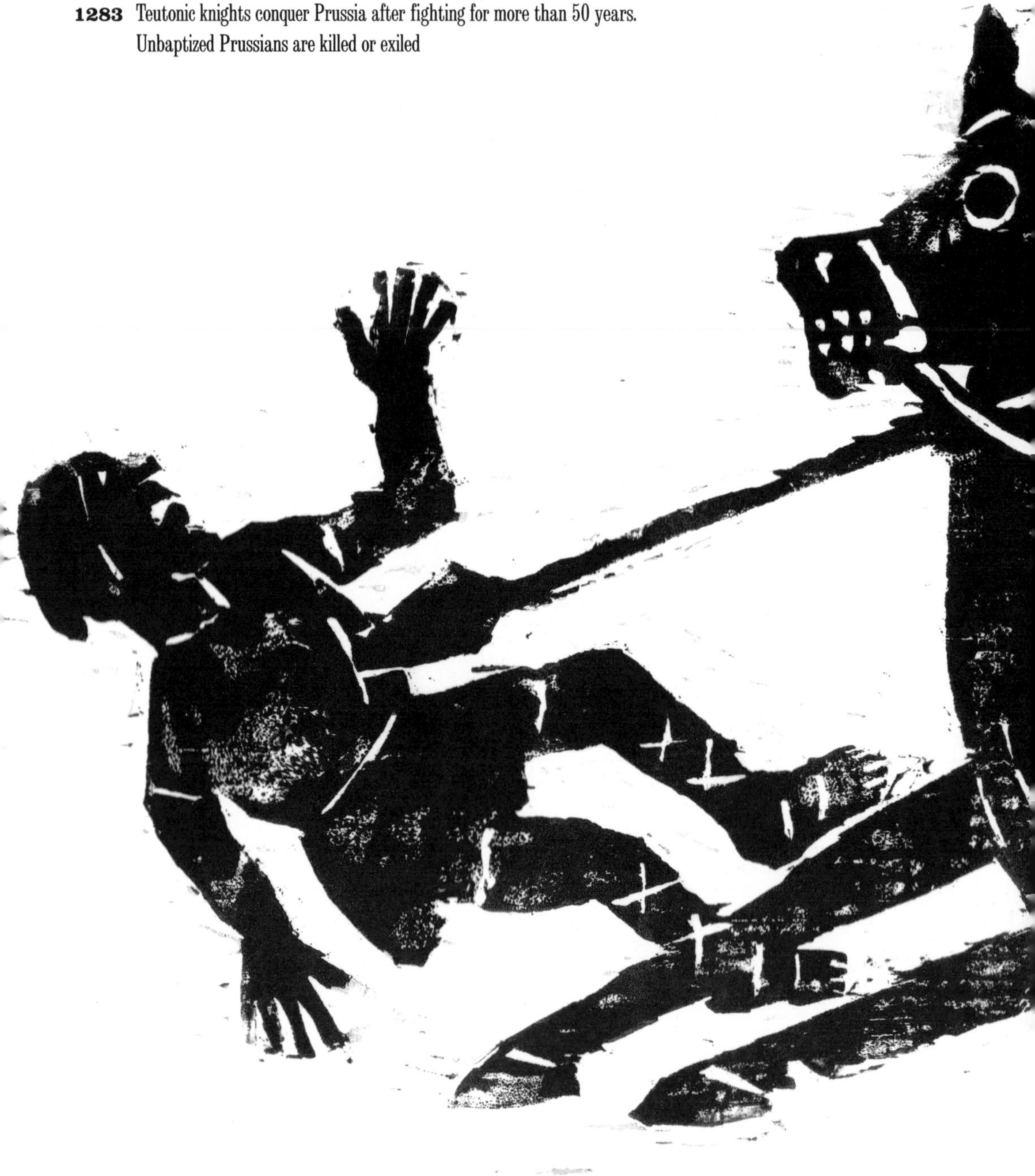

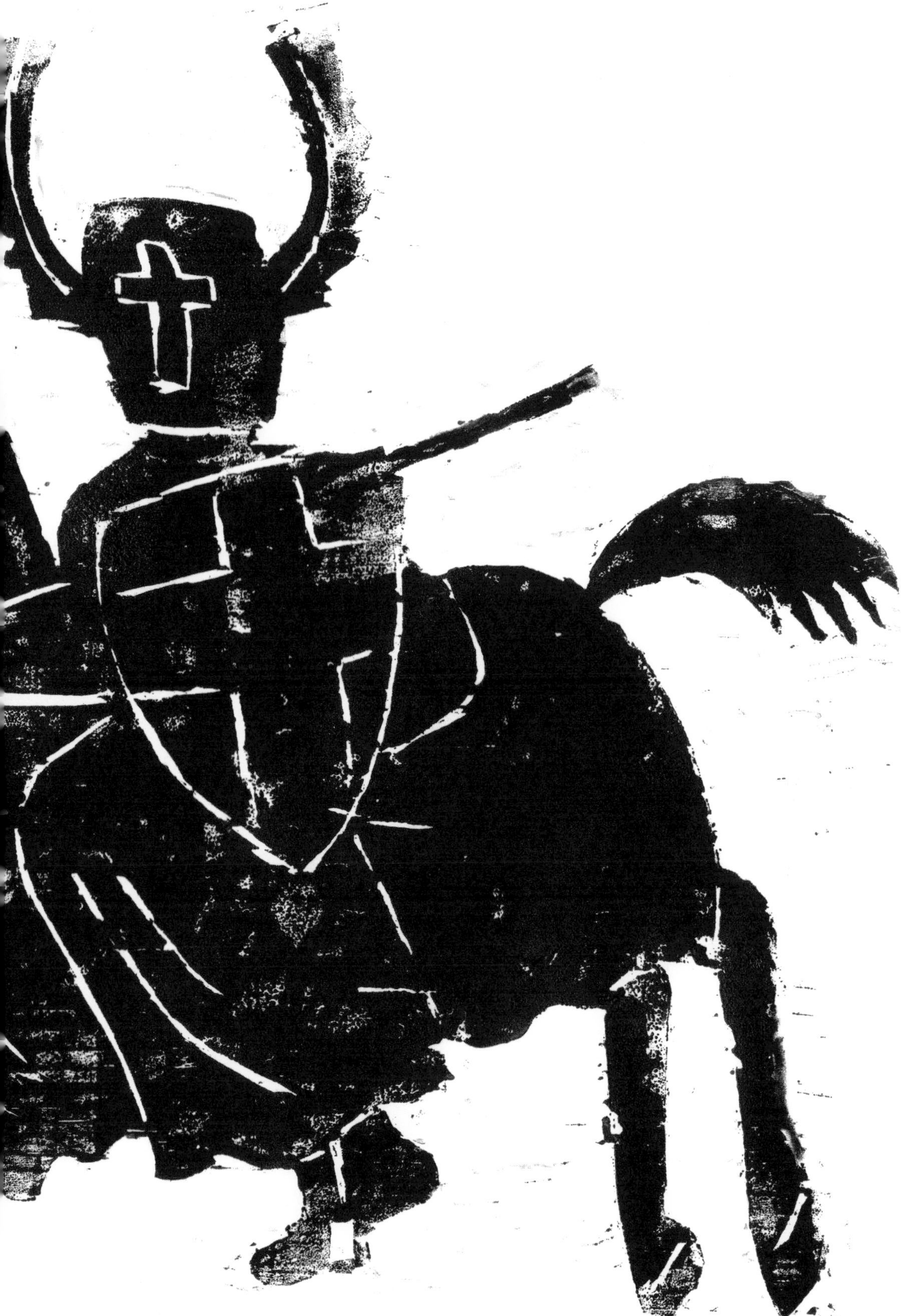

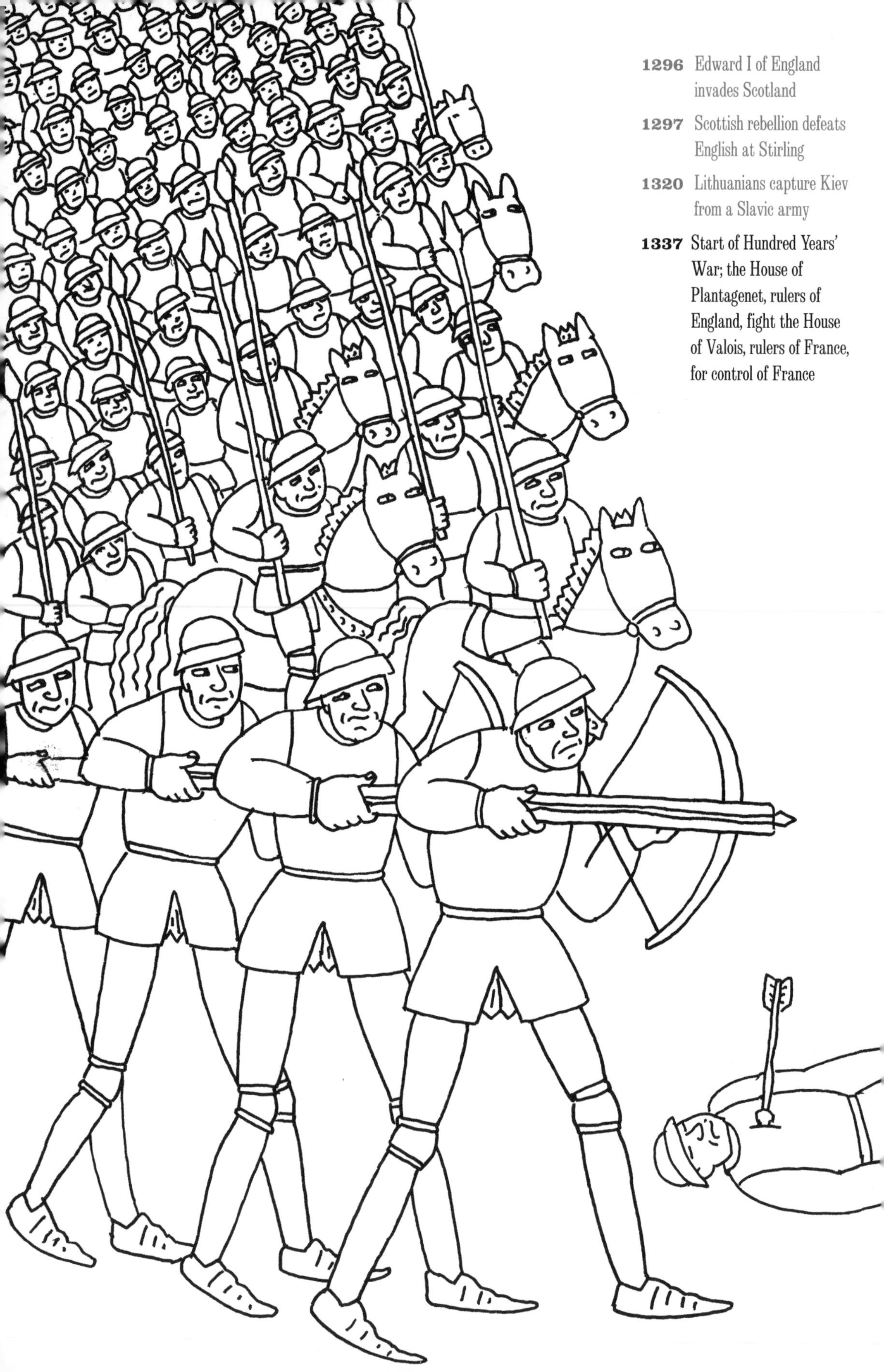

1296 Edward I of England invades Scotland

1297 Scottish rebellion defeats English at Stirling

1320 Lithuanians capture Kiev from a Slavic army

1337 Start of Hundred Years' War; the House of Plantagenet, rulers of England, fight the House of Valois, rulers of France, for control of France

1343 Majapahit empire conquers Bali

1343 English war with Moors

1373 John of Gaunt leads English invasion of France

1381 Wat Tyler's Rebellion in England

1387 Isfahan battles the Muslim leader, Timur, who kills 70,000, building towers with their skulls

1389 Victory of Ottomans over Serbs and Bosnians

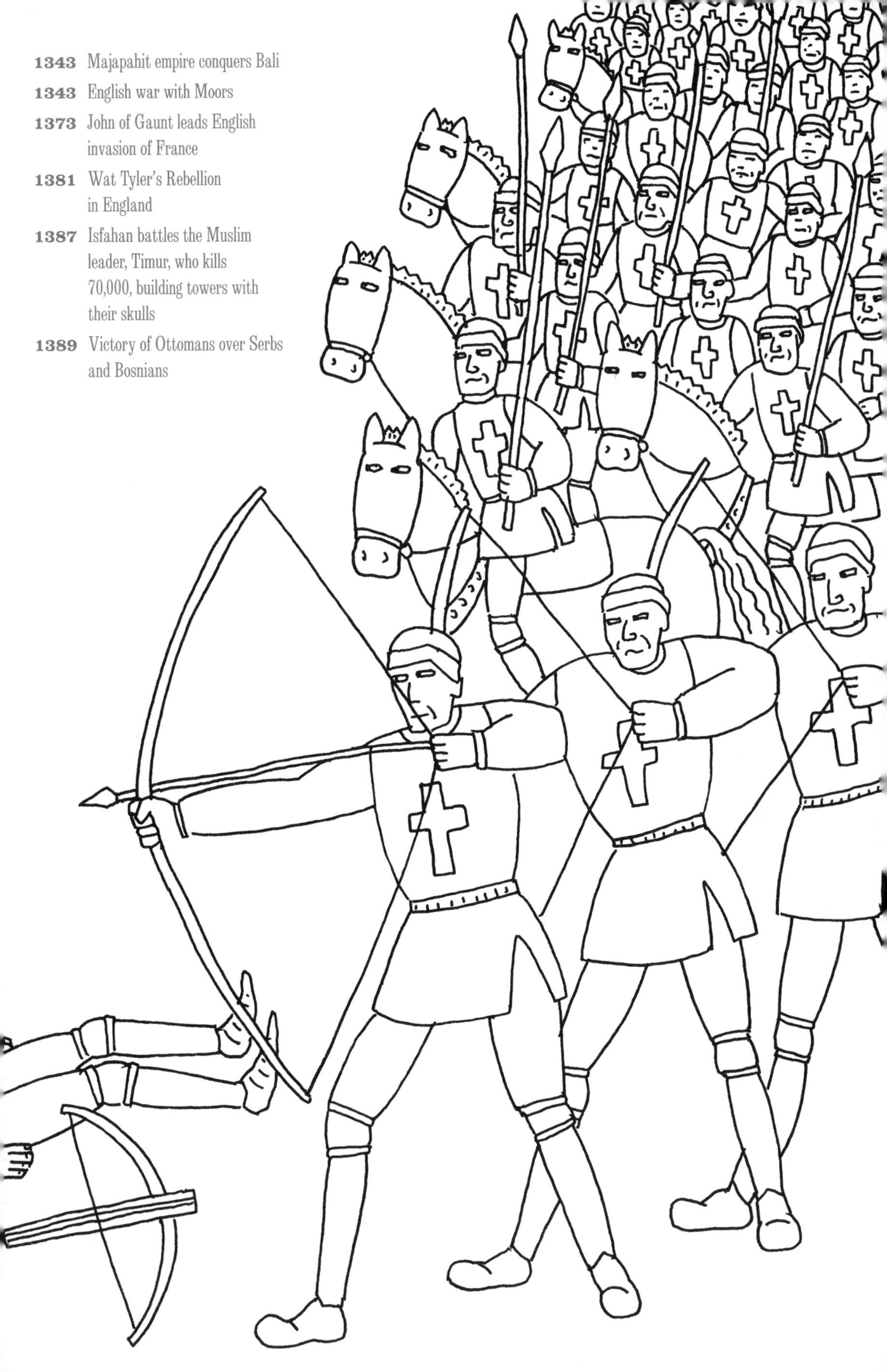

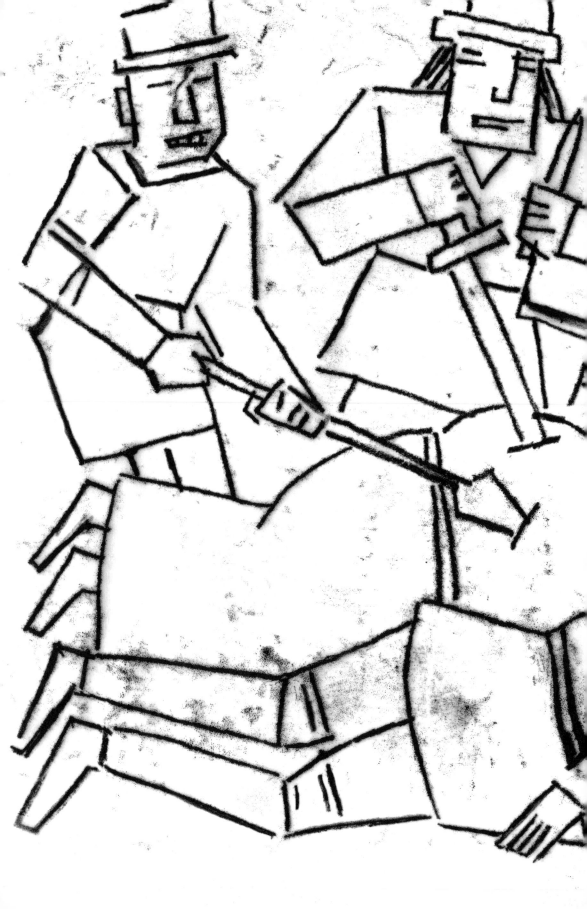

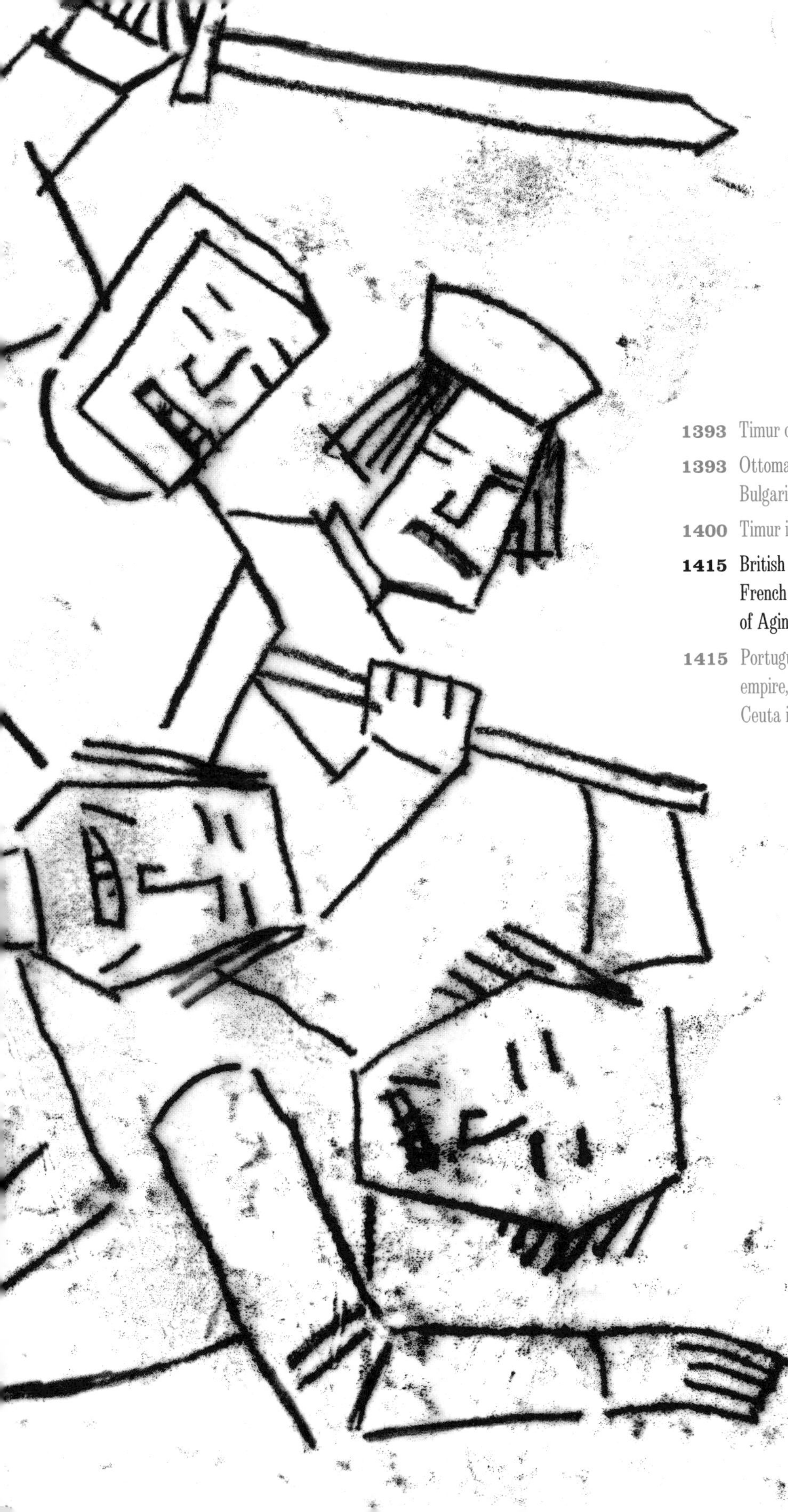

1393 Timur captures Baghdad

1393 Ottomans conquer Bulgaria

1400 Timur invades Syria

1415 British defeat French in Battle of Agincourt

1415 Portuguese begin their empire, capturing Ceuta in Morocco

1415 Jan Hus burned at the stake fighting a corrupt Church

1423 Start of Thirty Years' War between Milan and Florence

1428 In Mexico, the Aztec Empire begins conquering Atzcapotzalco.

1429 English siege of Orleans

1453 Ottoman Turks under Muhammad II take Constantinople

1455 Rival dynasties in England in a civil war, the War of the Roses

1471 Annamites invade Hindu state of Champa (South Vietnam)

1477 With the Battle of Nancy, Habsburgs acquire the Netherlands

1496 Ottoman forces invade Montenegro

1515 France invades Italy and occupies Milan

1515 Turks occupy Syria

1515 The Spanish forces occupy Cuba

1519 Hernando Cortés conquers Mexico

1525 Babur wins the First Battle of Panipat, founds Mongol Empire

1526 Ottomans invade Hungary, win a victory
at the Battle of Mohács

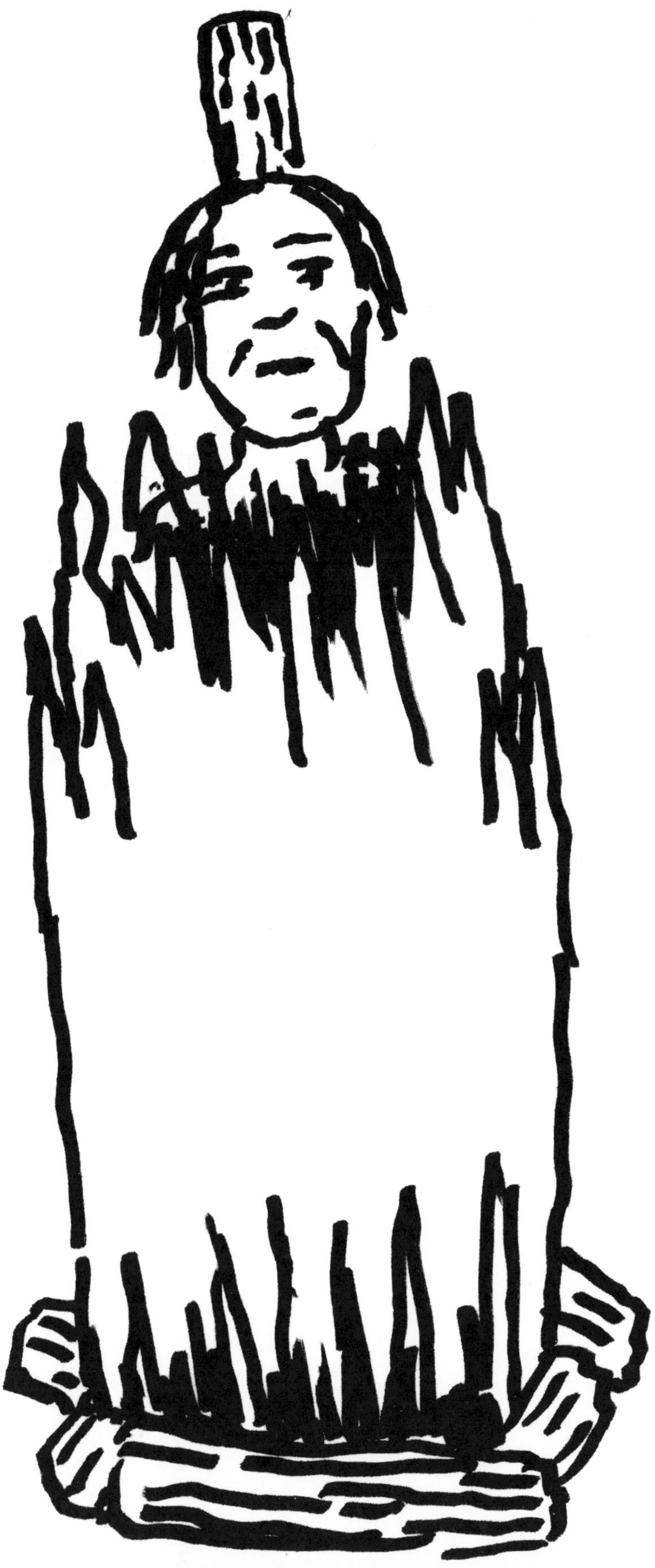

1527 Muslims conquer Christian Nubia in southern Egypt after a seven-year war

1532 Pizarro conquers Inca Empire and executes the last Inca emperor

1542 Peasants' War in Germany

1542 English conquer Scots at the Battle of Solway Moss

1549 Kett's Rebellion in England

1550 French take Boulogne from English who also leave Scotland

1557 Queen Mary of England declares war on France

1557 Spain defeats French at St. Quentin

1558 Ivan the Terrible of Russia invades Lithuania

1571 Austrian war with Turks

1581 Swedes recapture Estonia

1588 The Spanish Armada, a fleet of 130 ships, attempts to invade England. It is defeated by the English naval force and is a great victory for Queen Elizabeth I

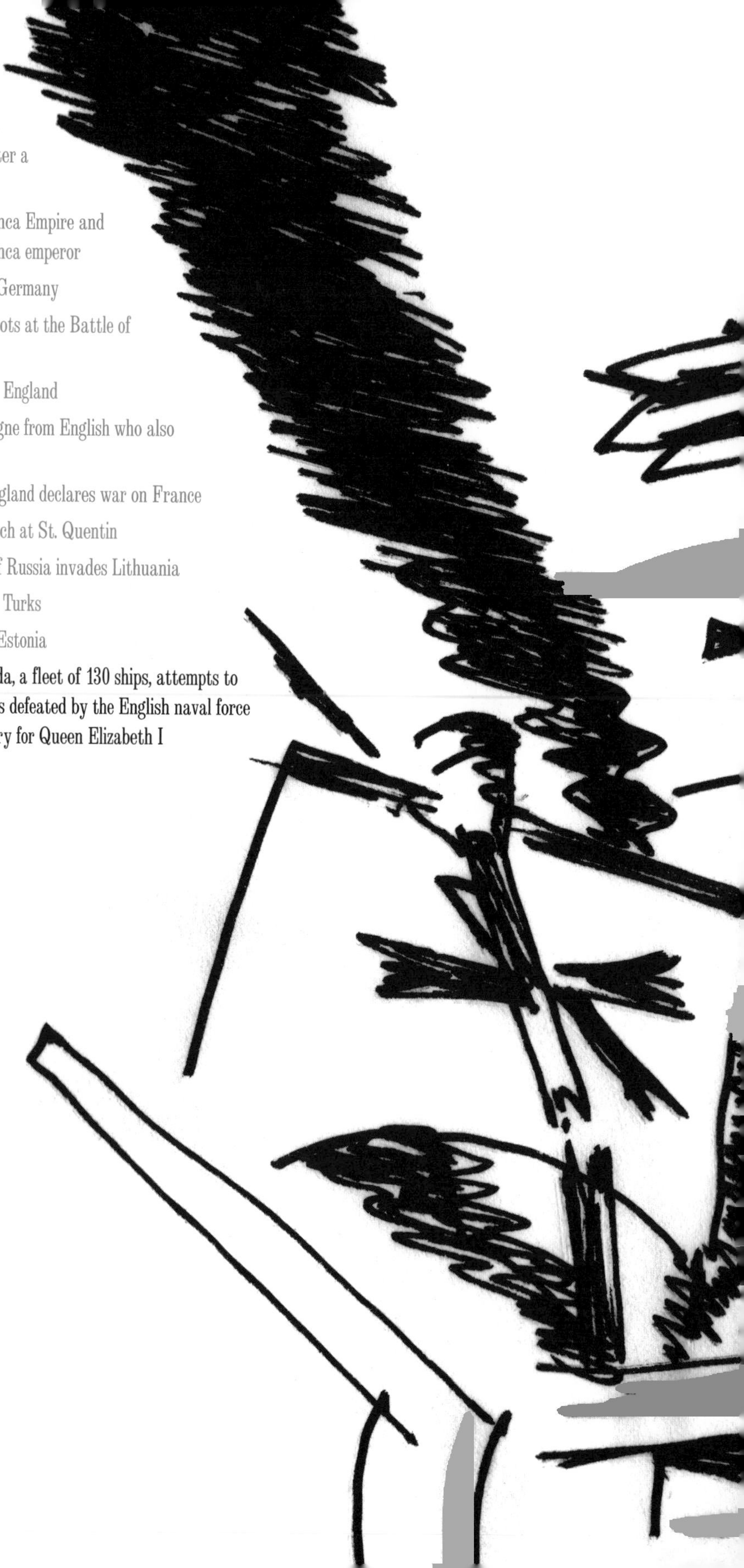

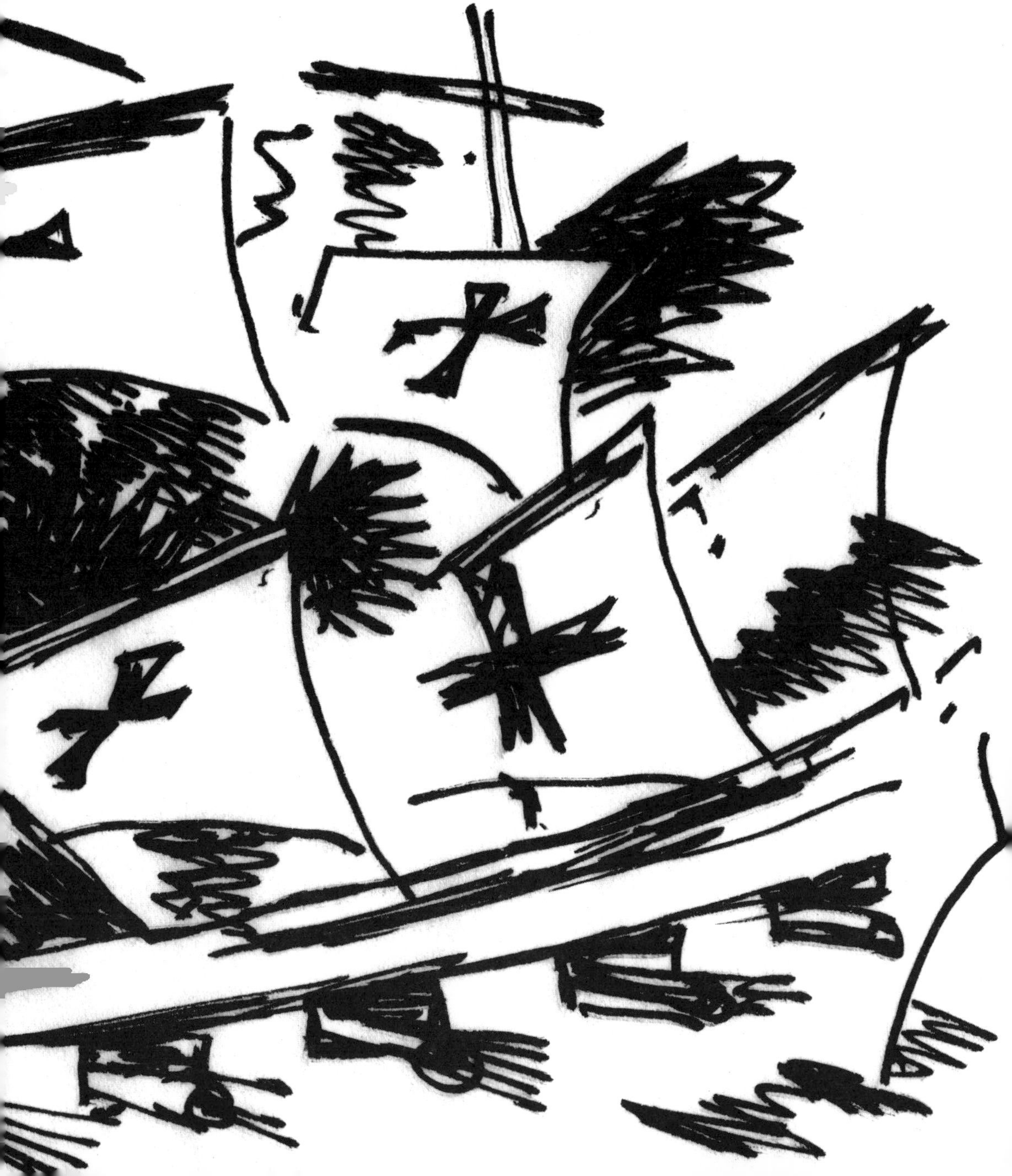

1592 Korea invaded by Japan

1593 Start of the Hungarian Thirteen Years' War with Turkey

1611 The Kalmar War pits Sweden against Denmark over control of the Baltic states

1618 Bohemian revolt against Habsburg control. Thirty Years' War begins

1619 Russia invades Beijing

1622 In Virginia, Native American attack leaves 240 English colonists dead

1630 Dutch conquer Brazil

1637 500 Native Americans killed in a Puritan attack on Pequot village

1648 The Fronde, a series of civil wars in France, occurs in the midst of the
Franco-Spanish War.

1650 Oliver Cromwell defeats Scottish uprising at the Battle of Dunbar

1652 Anglo-Dutch War declared by the English

1655 Sweden conquers Warsaw and Cracow

1659 War between Dutch settlers and the Khoisan, southern African herders

1664 Second Anglo-Dutch War. English capture New Amsterdam, rename it New York

1667 War of Devolution. France conquers the Habsburg-controlled Spanish Netherlands

1676 English settlers defeat New England Native Americans

1683 Siege of Vienna by Ottomans fails

1688 "Glorious" Revolution in England. Mary and William of Orange installed
as monarchs

1688 French provoke rebellion overthrowing King Narai of Siam

1697 Start of Russia's conquest of Siberia

1700 Great Northern War, between Russia and Sweden. Russia wins

1700 Sweden invades Denmark and occupies Copenhagen

1710 War between Ottomans and Russia ending in Ottoman victory the following year

1717 Britain, France and the Netherlands contain expansion of Spain

1720 Warfare between French and Spanish forces in Florida and Texas

1733 War of the Polish Succession

1737 New Russian war with the Ottomans

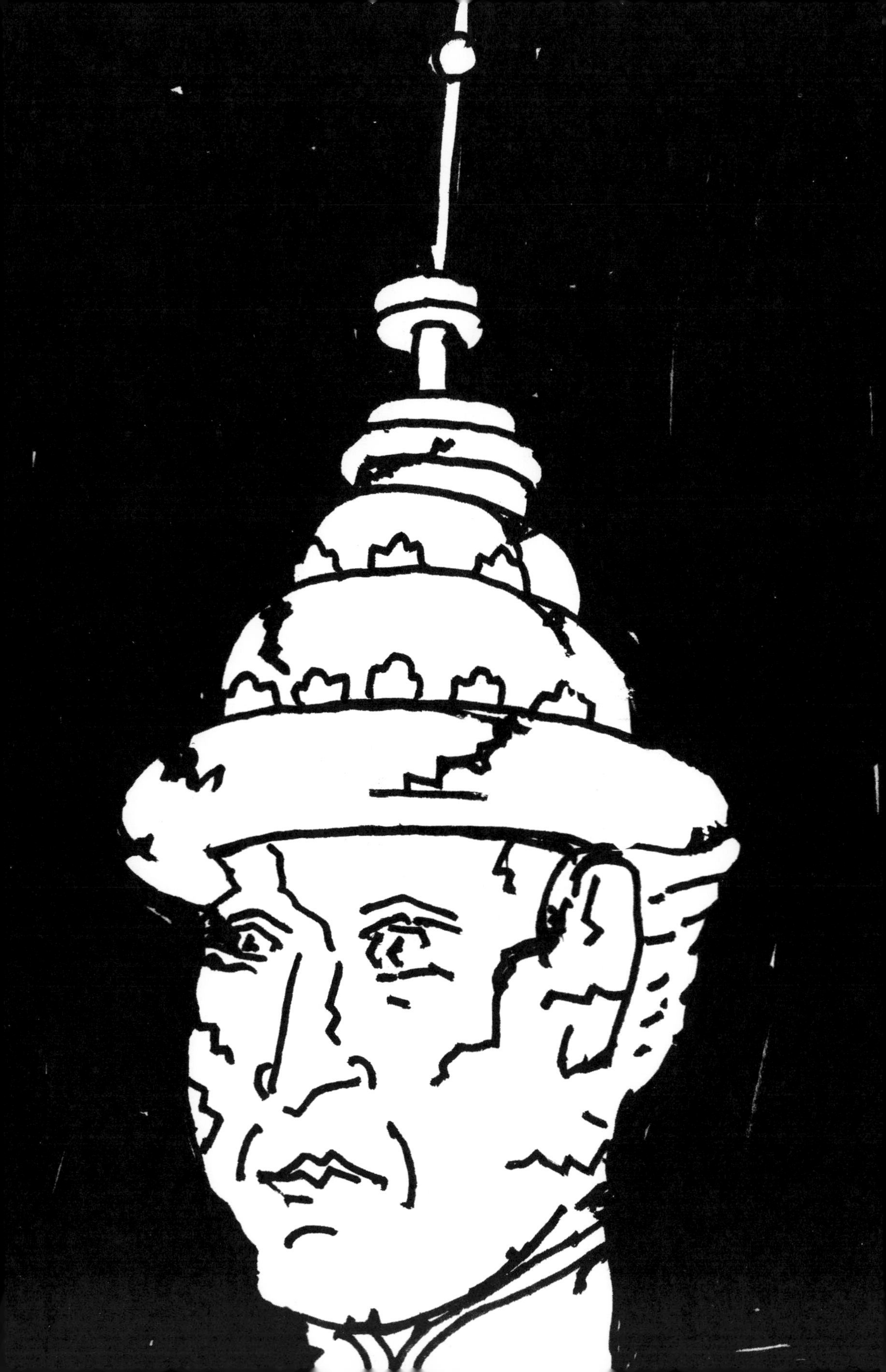

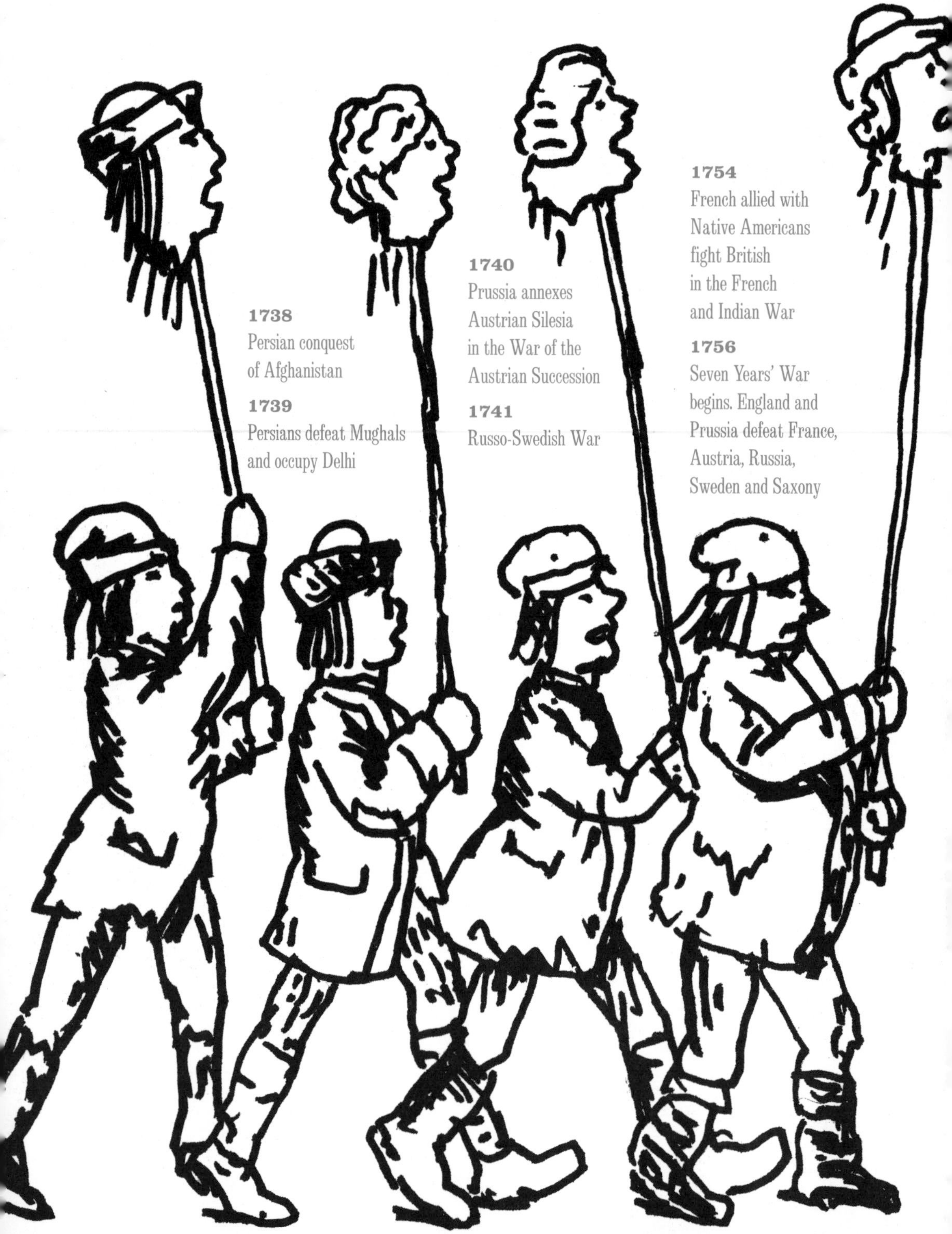

1738
Persian conquest of Afghanistan

1739
Persians defeat Mughals and occupy Delhi

1740
Prussia annexes Austrian Silesia in the War of the Austrian Succession

1741
Russo-Swedish War

1754
French allied with Native Americans fight British in the French and Indian War

1756
Seven Years' War begins. England and Prussia defeat France, Austria, Russia, Sweden and Saxony

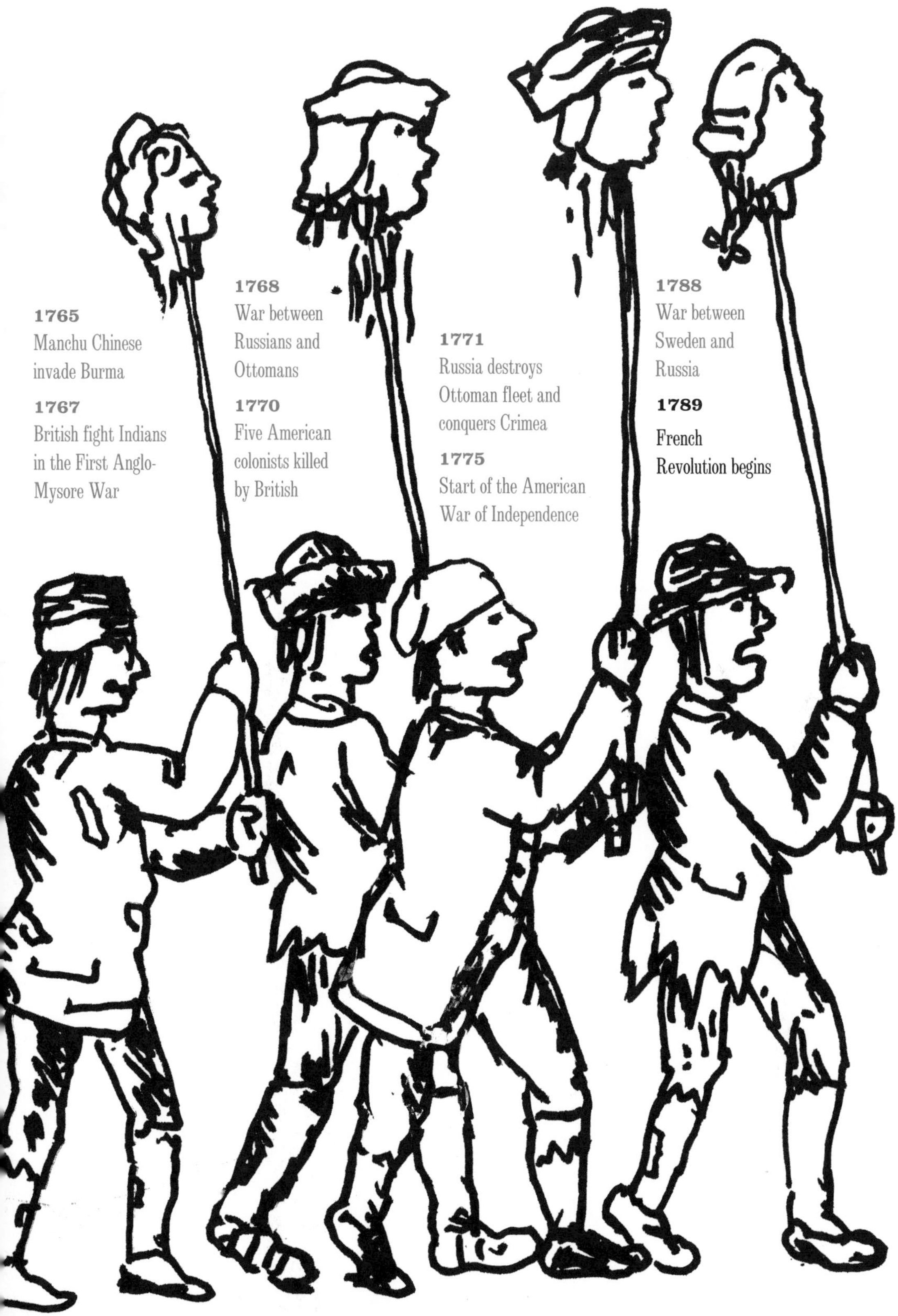

1765
Manchu Chinese invade Burma

1767
British fight Indians in the First Anglo-Mysore War

1768
War between Russians and Ottomans

1770
Five American colonists killed by British

1771
Russia destroys Ottoman fleet and conquers Crimea

1775
Start of the American War of Independence

1788
War between Sweden and Russia

1789
French Revolution begins

Desiderius Erasmus

The Complaint of Peace

This excerpt from the 1521 treatise was translated by Thomas Paynell.

Let [one] be persuaded that the best method of enriching and improving his realm is not by taking from the territory of others, but by meliorating the condition of his own. When the expediency of war is discussed, let him not listen to the counsels of young ministers, who are pleased with the false glory of war, without considering its calamities, of which, from their age, it is impossible that they should have had personal experience. Neither let him consult those who have an interest in disturbing the public tranquility and who are fed and fattened by the sufferings of the people. Let him take the advice of old men, whose integrity has been long tried, and who have shown that they have an unfeigned attachment to their country. Nor let him, to gratify the passions or sinister views of one or two violent or artful men, rashly enter on a war; for war, once engaged in, cannot be put an end to at discretion. A measure the most dangerous to the existence of a state as a war must be, should not be entered into by a king, by a minister, by a junta of ambitious, avaricious or revengeful men, but by the full and unanimous consent of the whole people.

The causes of war are to be cut up root and branch, on their first and slightest appearance. Men must not be too zealous about a phantom called national glory; often inconsistent with individual happiness. Gentle behavior on one side will tend to secure it on the other; but the insolence of a haughty minister may give unpardonable offense, and be dearly paid for by the sufferings of the nation over which he domineers.

There are occasions when, if peace can be had in no other way, it must be purchased. It can scarcely be purchased too dearly, if you take into the account how much treasure you must inevitably expend in war; and what is of infinitely greater consequence than treasure, how many of the people's lives you save by peace. Though the cost be great, yet war would certainly cost you more; besides, (what is above all, price) the blood of men, the blood of your own fellow-citizens and subjects, whose lives you are bound, by every tie of duty, to preserve, instead of lavishing away in prosecuting schemes of false policy, and cruel, selfish, villainous ambition. Only form a fair estimate of the quantity of mischief and misery of every kind and degree which you escape, and the sum of happiness you preserve in all the walks of private life, among all the tender relations of parents, husbands, children, among those whose poverty alone makes them soldiers, the wretched instruments of involuntary bloodshed; form but this estimate, and you will never repent the highest price you can pay for peace.

While the king does his duty as the guardian and preserver, instead of the destroyer, of the people committed to his charge, let the right reverend the bishops do their duty likewise. Let the priests be priests indeed; preachers of peace and goodwill, and not the instigators of war, for the sake of pleasing a corrupt minister, in whose hands are livings, stalls and mitres; let the whole body of the clergy remember the truly evangelical duties of their profession, and let the grave professors of theology in our universities, or wherever else they teach divinity, remember to teach nothing as men-pleasers unworthy of Christ. Let all the clergy, however they may differ in rank, order, sect or persuasion, unite to cry down war, and discountenance it through the nation, by zealously and faithfully arraigning it from the pulpit. In the public functions of their several churches, in their private conversation and intercourse with the laity, let them be constantly employed in the Christian, benevolent, humane work of preaching, recommending and inculcating, peace. If, after all their efforts, the clergy cannot prevent the breaking out of war, let them never give it the slightest approbation, directly or indirectly, let them never give countenance to it by their presence at its silly parade or bloody proceedings, let them never pay the smallest respect to any great patron or prime minister, or courtier, who is the author or adviser of a state of affairs so contrary to their holy profession, and to every duty and principle of the Christian religion, as is a state of war.

Let the clergy agree to refuse burial in consecrated ground to all who are slain in battle. If there be any good men among the slain, and certainly there are very few, they will not lose the reward of Christians in heaven, because they had not what is called Christian burial. But the worthless, of whom the majority of warriors consists, will have one cause of that silly vanity and self-liking which attends and recommends their profession more than anything else entirely removed, when sepulchral honors are denied, after all the glory of being knocked on the head in battle, in the noble endeavor to kill a fellow-creature.

I am speaking all along of those wars which Christians wage with Christians, on trifling and unjustifiable occasions. I think very differently of wars, bona fide, just and necessary, such as are, in a strict sense of those words, purely defensive, such as with an honest and affectionate zeal for the country, repel the violence of invaders, and, at the hazard of life, preserve the public tranquility.

But in the present state of things, the clergy (for of their conduct I proceed to speak) so far from acting as servants of Christ, in the manner I have recommended, do not hesitate to hang up flags, standards, banners and other trophies of war, brought from the field of carnage, as ornaments of churches and great cathedrals. These trophies shall be all stained and smeared with the blood of men, for whom Christ shed his most precious blood, and shall be hung in the aisles of the churches, among the tombs and images of apostles and martyrs, as if in future it were to be reckoned a mark of sanctity not to suffer martyrdom, but to inflict it; not to lay down one's life for the truth, but to take away the life of others for worldly purposes of vanity and avarice. It would be quite sufficient if the bloody rags were hung up in some corner of the Exchange or kept, as curiosities in a chest or closet, out of

sight; disgraceful monuments they are of human depravity. The church, which ought to be kept perfectly pure, and emblematic of the purest of religions, should not be defiled with anything stained with the blood of man, shed by the hand of man alienated, as is clear by the very act, both from Christ and from nature.

But you argue in defense of this indecent practice of hanging up flags or colors, as they are called, in churches, that the ancients used to deposit the monuments of their victories in the temples of their gods. It is true, but what were their gods but demons, delighting in blood and impurity? Not the God, who is of purer eyes than to behold iniquity. Never let priests have anything to do with war, unless it is to put an end to it, and promote love and reconciliation. If the clergy were but unanimous in such sentiments, if they would inculcate them everywhere, there is no doubt, notwithstanding the great power of the secular arm, that their authority, personal and professional, would have a preponderance, against the influence of courts and ministers of state, and thus prevent war, the calamity of human nature.

But if there is a fatal propensity in the human heart to war, if the dreadful disease is interwoven with the constitution of man, so that it cannot abstain from war, why is not vent given to the virulence in exertions against the common enemy of Christianity, the unbelieving Turk? Yet—even here let me pause—is not the Turk a man—a brother? Then it were far better to allure him by gentle, kind, and friendly treatment, by exhibiting the beauty of our Christian religion in the innocence of our lives, than by attacking him with the drawn sword, as if he were a savage brute, without a heart to feel, or a reasoning faculty to be persuaded. Nevertheless, if we must of necessity go to war, as I said before, it is certainly a less evil to contend with an infidel, than that Christians should mutually harass and destroy their own fraternity. If charity will not cement their hearts, certainly one common enemy may unite their hands, and though this may not be a cordial unity, yet it will be better than a real rupture.

Upon the whole it must be said, that the first and most important step toward peace, is sincerely to desire it. They who once love peace in their hearts, will eagerly seize every opportunity of establishing or recovering it. All obstacles to it they will despise or remove, all hardships and difficulties they will bear with patience, so long as they keep this one great blessing (including as it does so many others) whole and entire. On the contrary, men, in our times, go out of their way to seek occasions of war; and whatever makes for peace, they run down in their sophistical speeches, or even basely conceal from the public; but whatever tends to promote their favorite war system, they industriously exaggerate and inflame, not scrupling to propagate lies of the most mischievous kind, false or garbled intelligence and the grossest misrepresentation of the enemy.

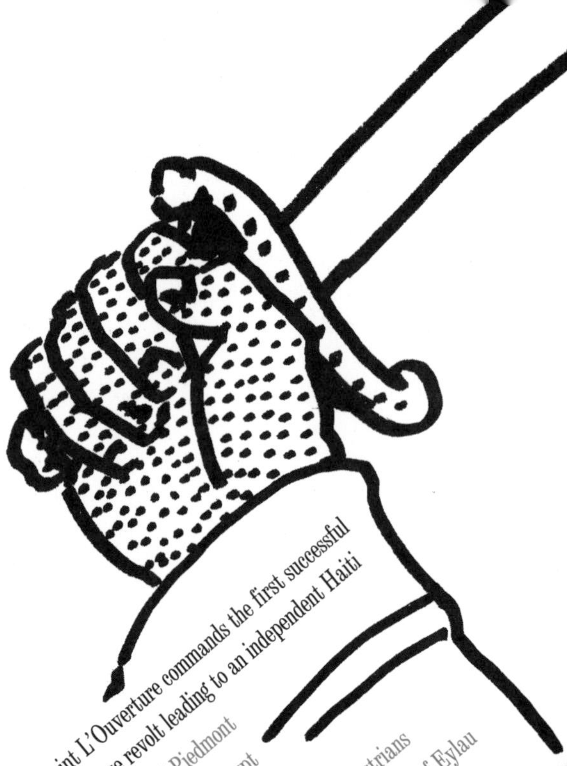

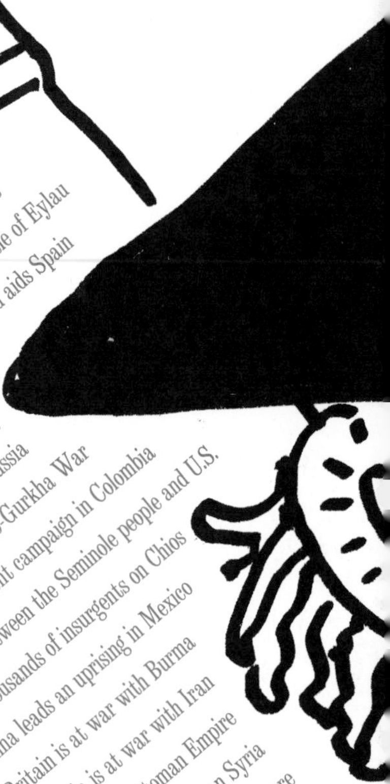

1791 Toussaint L'Ouverture commands the first successful slave revolt leading to an independent Haiti

1792 War of the First Coalition. France at war with Austria, Prussia and Piedmont

1798 British, under Horatio Nelson, defeat French in Egypt

1801 War between Tripoli and U.S. **1801** The Battle of Copenhagen

1805 Napoleonic Wars. With the Battle of Austerlitz, Napoleon defeats Russians and Austrians

1807 Napoleon defeats Russia in the Battle of Eylau

1808 Peninsular War. France invades Spain. England aids Spain

1808 Russia occupies Finland

1812 War of 1812. Britain attacks American navy

1812 Napoleon invades Russia

1815 British win Anglo-Gurkha War

1817 Spanish troops start a violent campaign in Colombia

1817 War between the Seminole people and U.S.

1822 Ottomans massacre thousands of insurgents on Chios

1823 Antonio López de Santa Anna leads an uprising in Mexico

1824 Britain is at war with Burma

1827 Russia is at war with Iran

1828 Russia declares war on Ottoman Empire

1831 Egyptians conquer Ottoman Syria

1832 The Battle of Bad Axe. U.S. troops massacre Chief Black Hawk and his people

1834 Belgian War of Independence

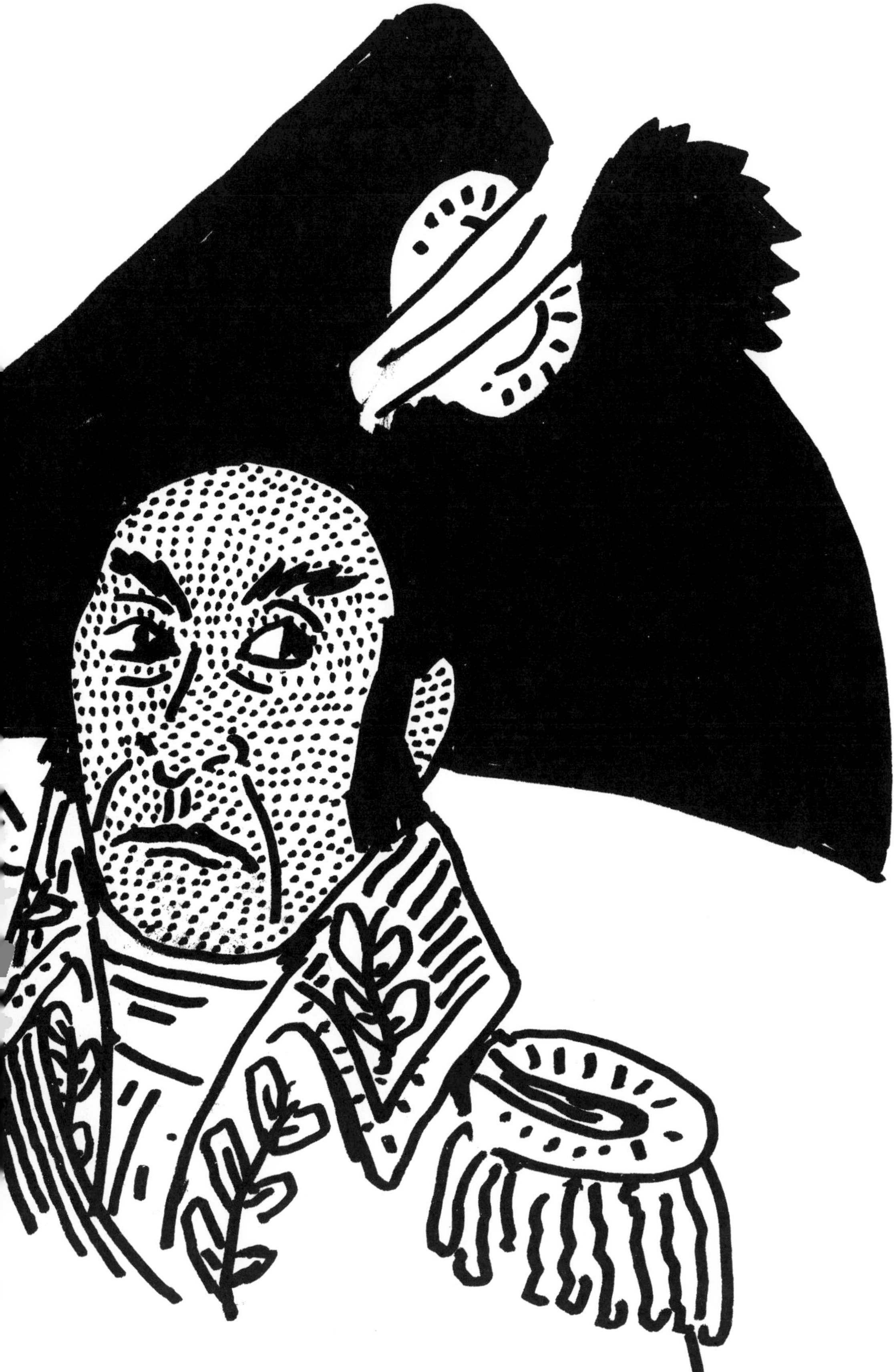

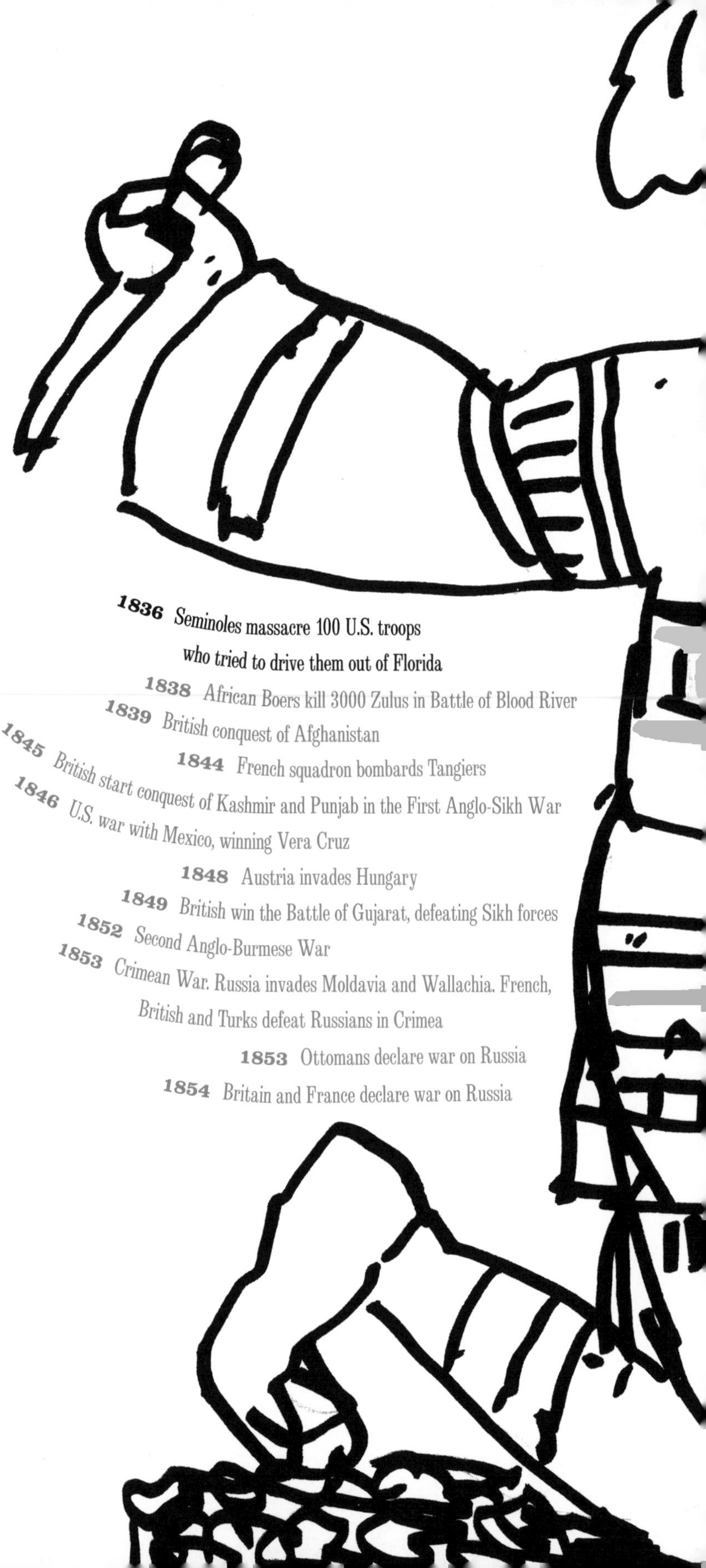

1836 Seminoles massacre 100 U.S. troops who tried to drive them out of Florida

1838 African Boers kill 3000 Zulus in Battle of Blood River

1839 British conquest of Afghanistan

1844 French squadron bombards Tangiers

1845 British start conquest of Kashmir and Punjab in the First Anglo-Sikh War

1846 U.S. war with Mexico, winning Vera Cruz

1848 Austria invades Hungary

1849 British win the Battle of Gujarat, defeating Sikh forces

1852 Second Anglo-Burmese War

1853 Crimean War. Russia invades Moldavia and Wallachia. French, British and Turks defeat Russians in Crimea

1853 Ottomans declare war on Russia

1854 Britain and France declare war on Russia

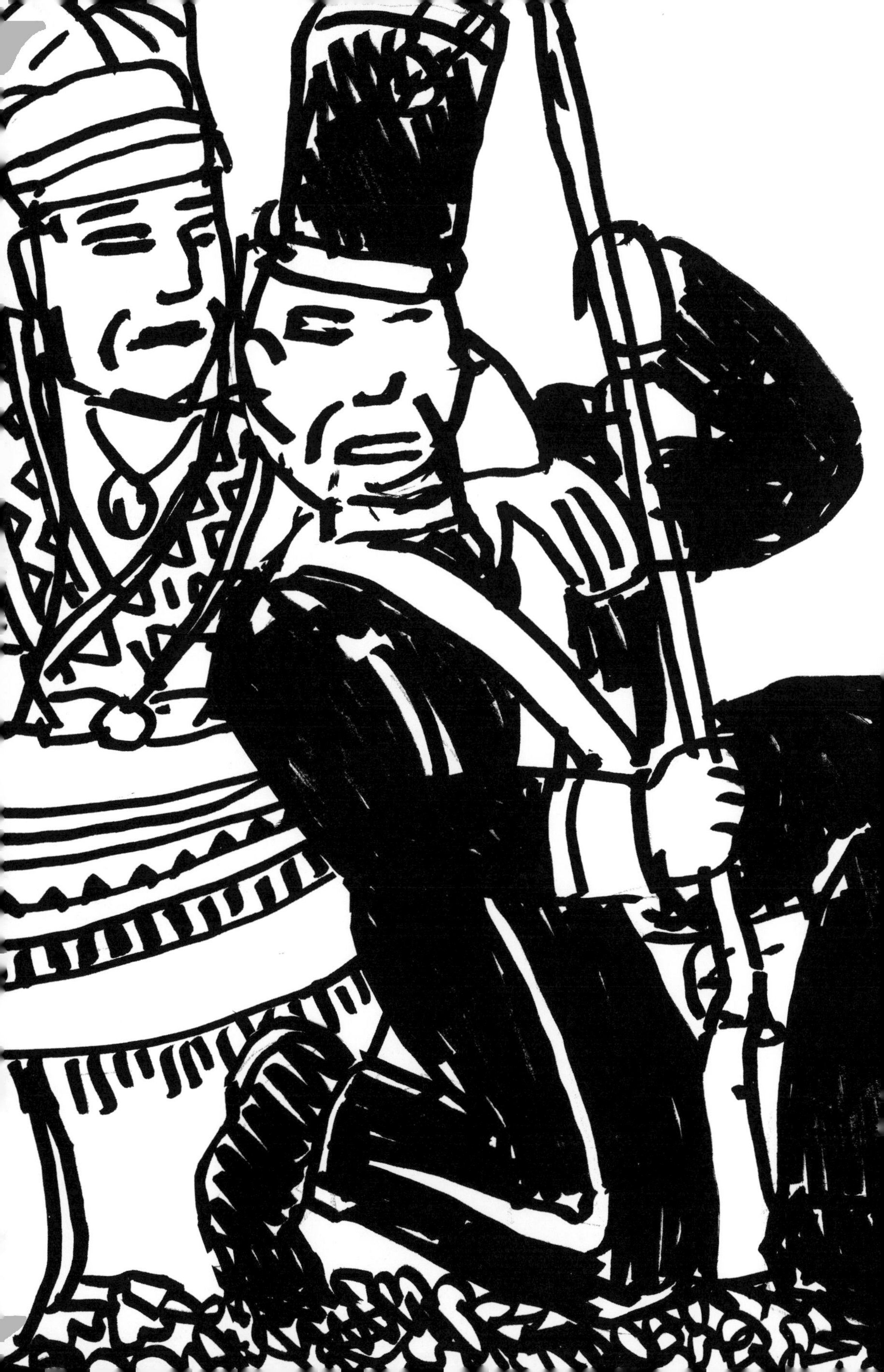

1856 Britain declares war on Persia after Persia's invasion of Afghanistan

1857 France and Britain declare war on China

1859 English and French occupy Beijing

1859 France declares war on Austria

1859 Austria and Prussia at war

1861 U.S. Civil War. Slave states secede from the Union. 750,000 Union and Confederate dead

1864 British, French, Dutch and U.S. navies bombard Japan to force it to open to trade

1864 Paraguayan War. Brazil, Argentina and Uruguay defeat Paraguay

1866 War between Prussia and Austria escalates

1866 Italy declares war on Austria, defeated at Battle of Custoza

1866 First Sioux War

1866 Peru declares war on Spain

1868 Britain defeats Ethiopia at the Battle of Aroge

1870 France declares war on Prussia. Napoleon III defeated by Prussians

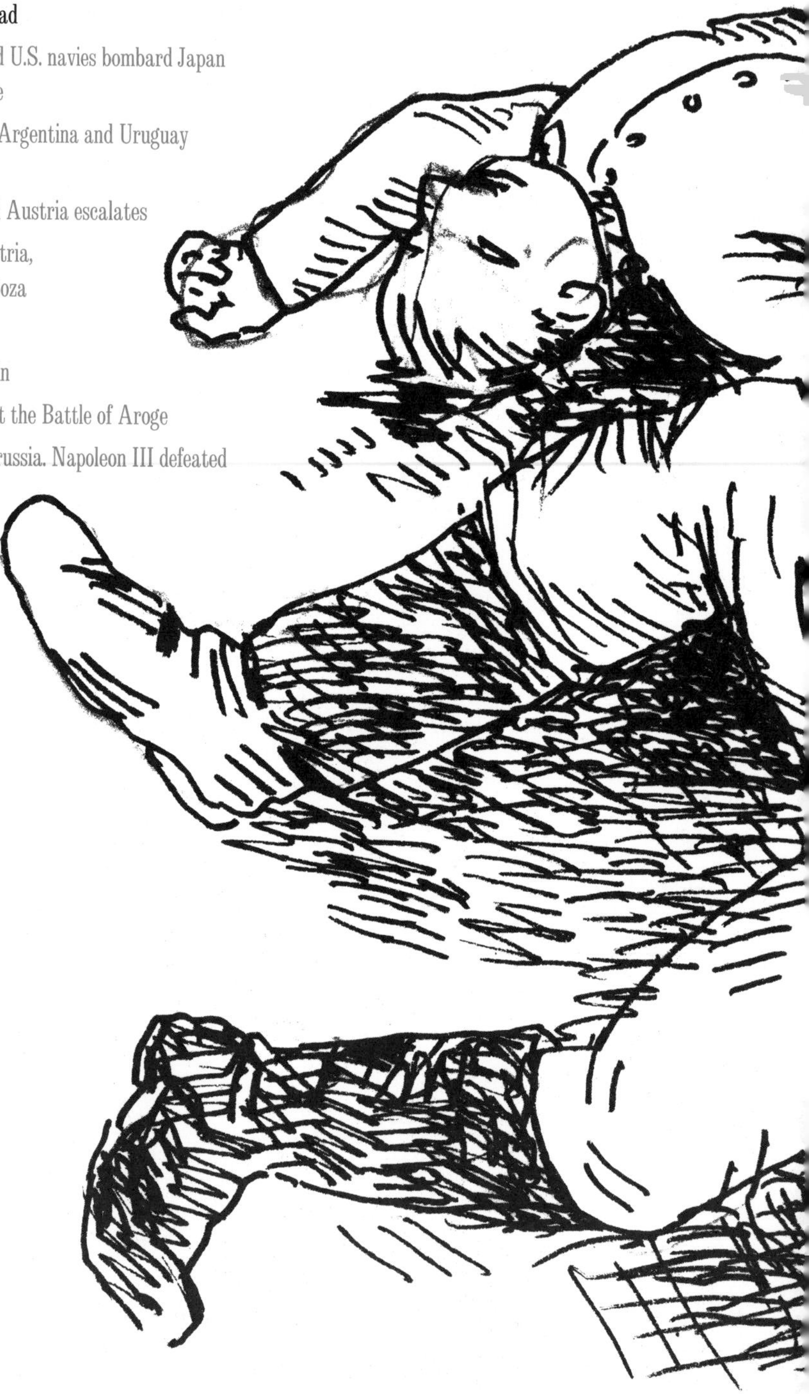

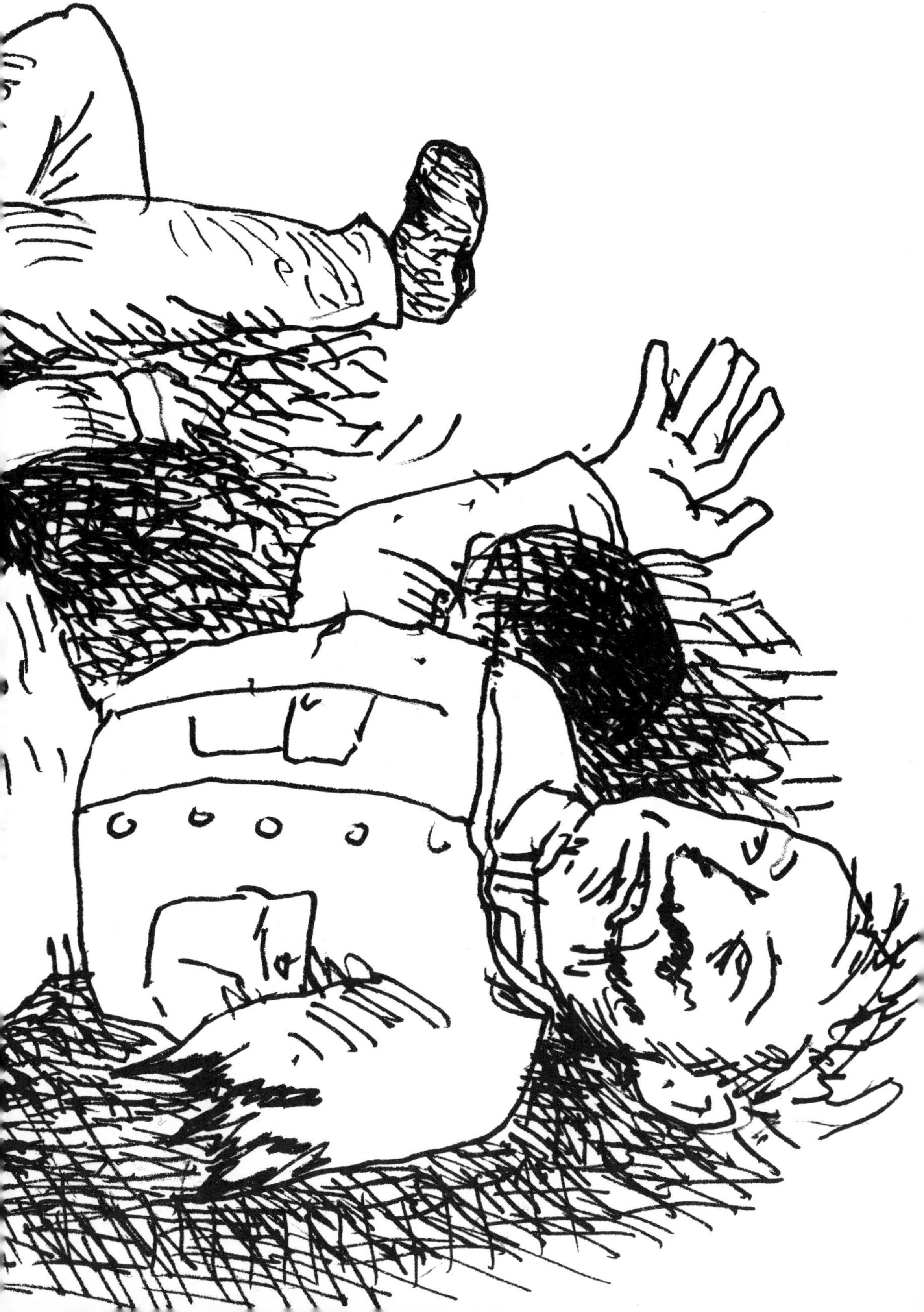

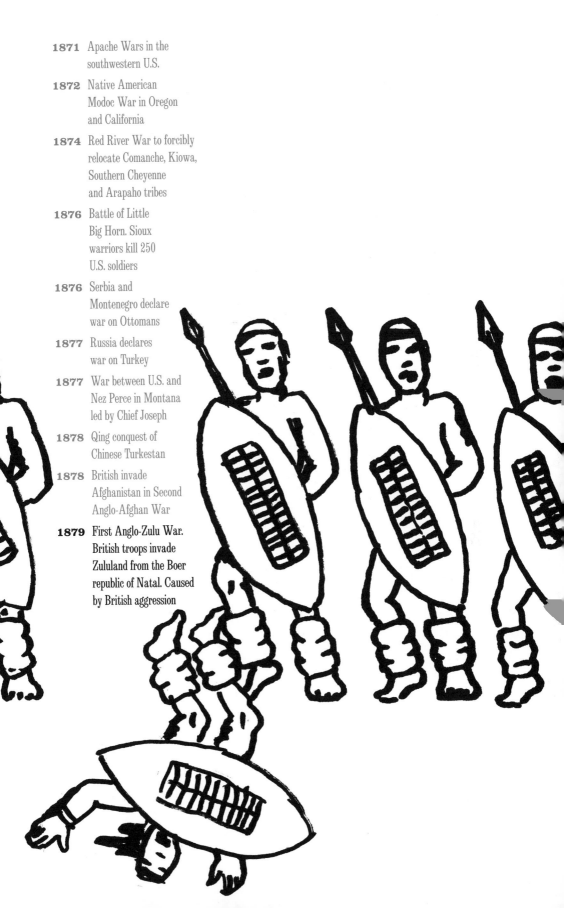

1871 Apache Wars in the southwestern U.S.

1872 Native American Modoc War in Oregon and California

1874 Red River War to forcibly relocate Comanche, Kiowa, Southern Cheyenne and Arapaho tribes

1876 Battle of Little Big Horn. Sioux warriors kill 250 U.S. soldiers

1876 Serbia and Montenegro declare war on Ottomans

1877 Russia declares war on Turkey

1877 War between U.S. and Nez Perce in Montana led by Chief Joseph

1878 Qing conquest of Chinese Turkestan

1878 British invade Afghanistan in Second Anglo-Afghan War

1879 First Anglo-Zulu War. British troops invade Zululand from the Boer republic of Natal. Caused by British aggression

1880 South African Boers fight the British and win

1880 Cuban revolt. Spain sends 250,000 troops

1886 Third Anglo-Burmese War. Britain takes upper Burma

1890 U.S. troops massacre 350 Sioux at Wounded Knee

1895 Battle of Weihaiwei. Japanese defeat Chinese

1898 Lord Kitchener wins the Battle of Omdurman, controlling Sudan

1898 U.S. destroys Spanish fleet in Manila Bay in the Spanish-American War

1899 Germans take Isangi and conquer Rwanda

1900 An anti-Western revolt in China called the Boxer Rebellion has a Chinese secret organization fight Western and Japanese influence. 32,000 Christians killed

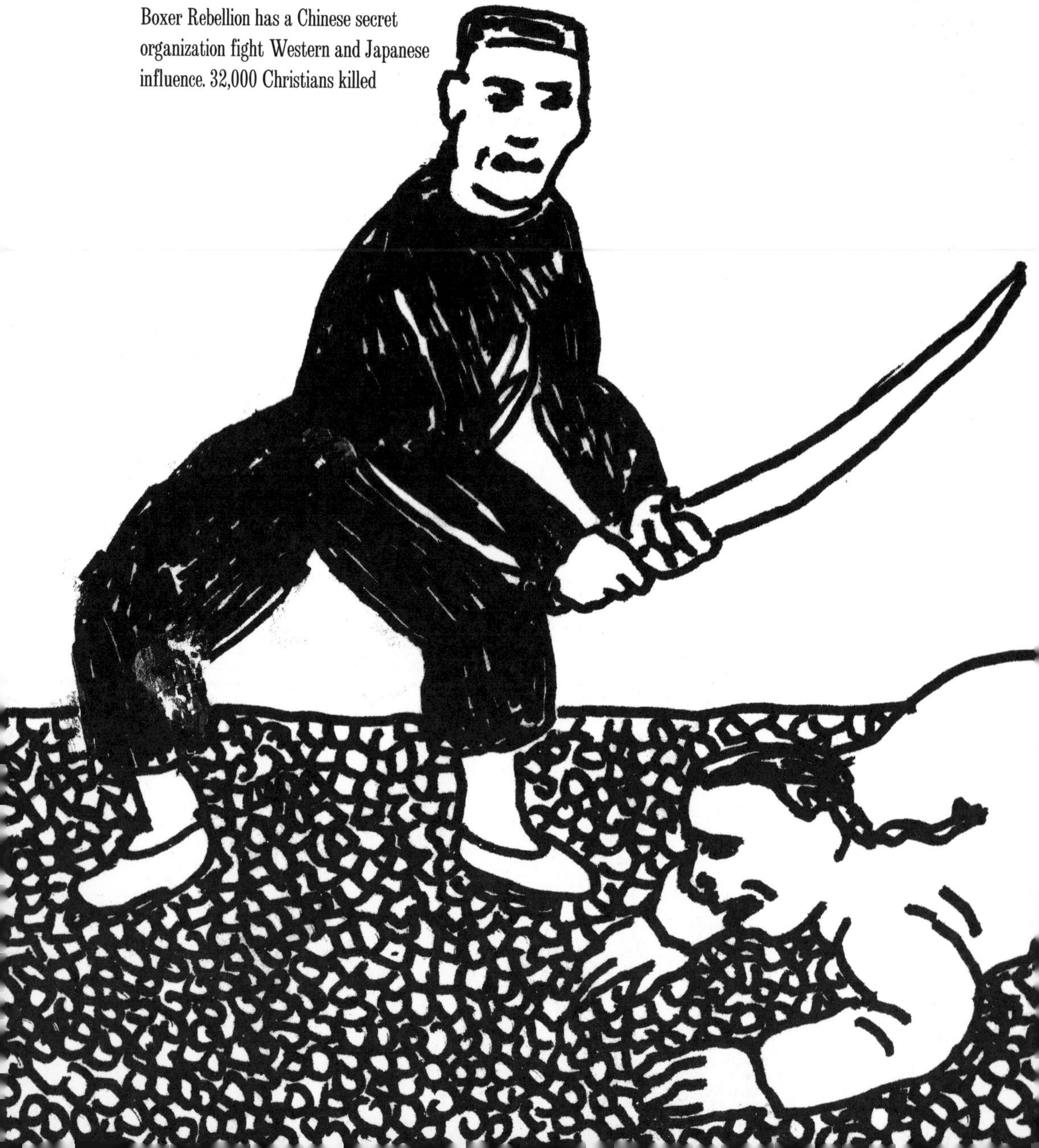

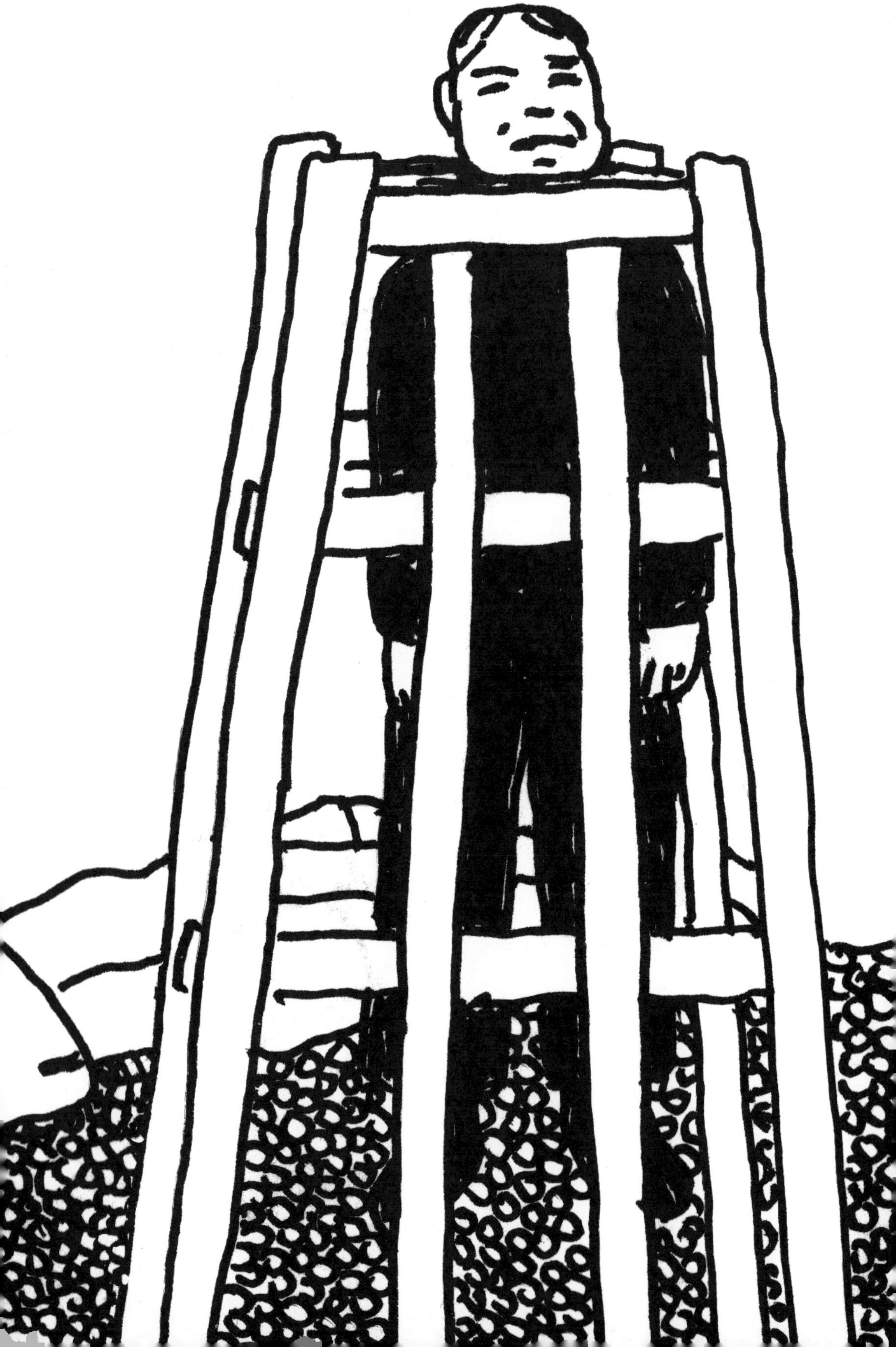

1903 Ottomans massacre 50,000 Bulgarians in Monastir

1904 Russo-Japanese War. Japanese defeat Russians at Telissu, China

1911 Mexican Revolution

1911 Chinese Revolution; Republic of China declared

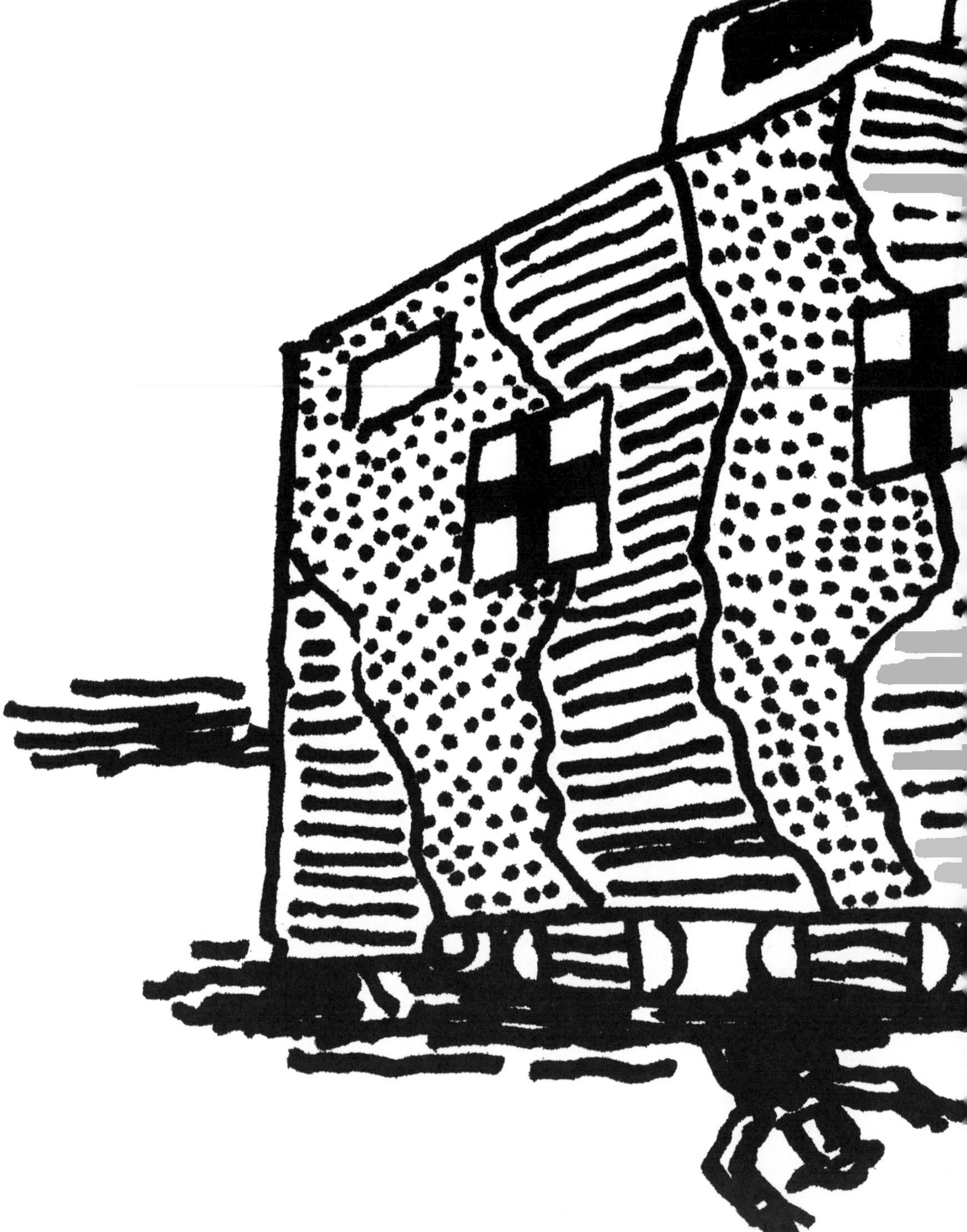

1912 Balkan League takes most European Ottoman territories in the First Balkan War

1912 Nicaraguan Civil War. U.S. military intervenes

1914 World War I begins. Ottomans, Germans and Austrians vs. British, French and Russians

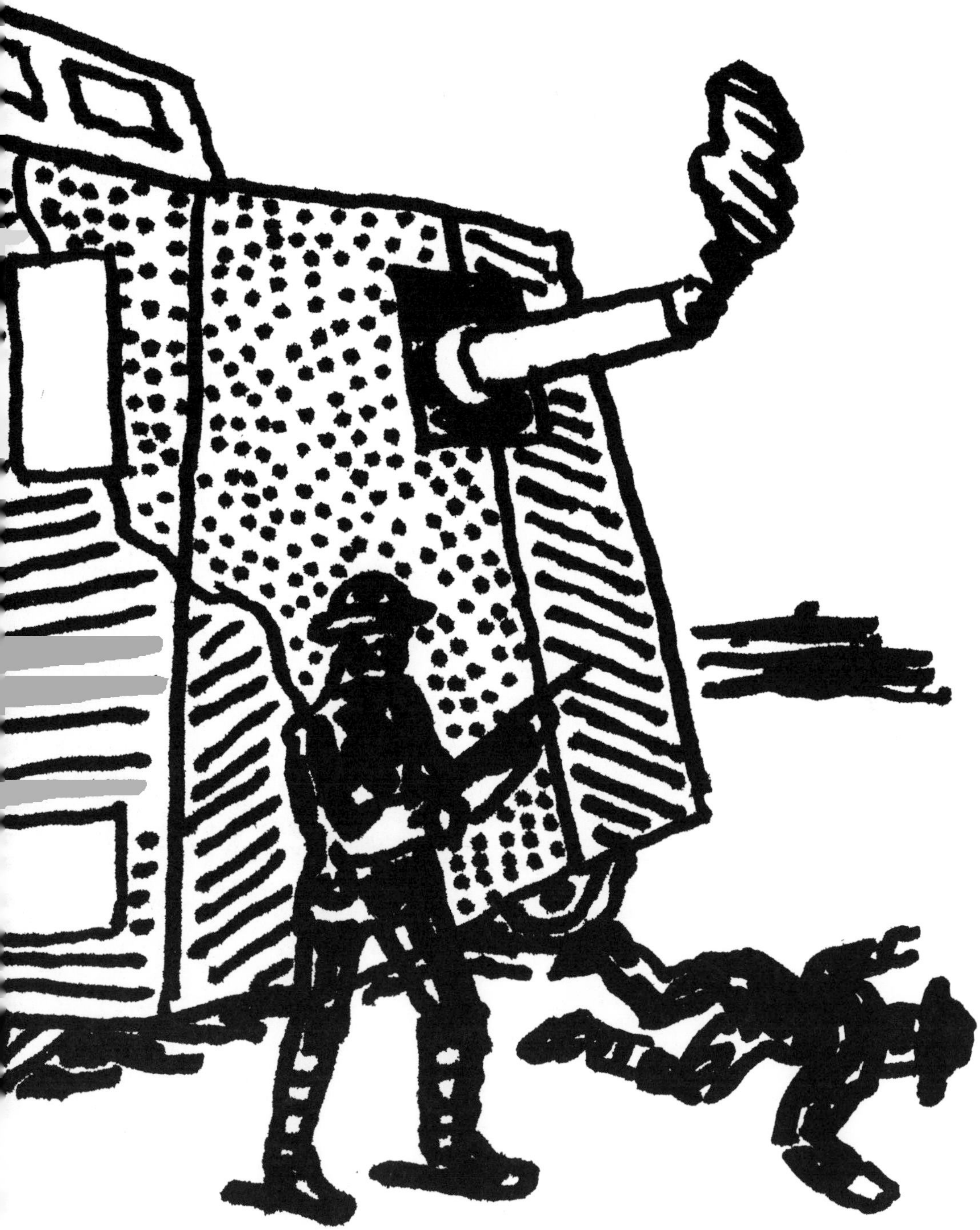

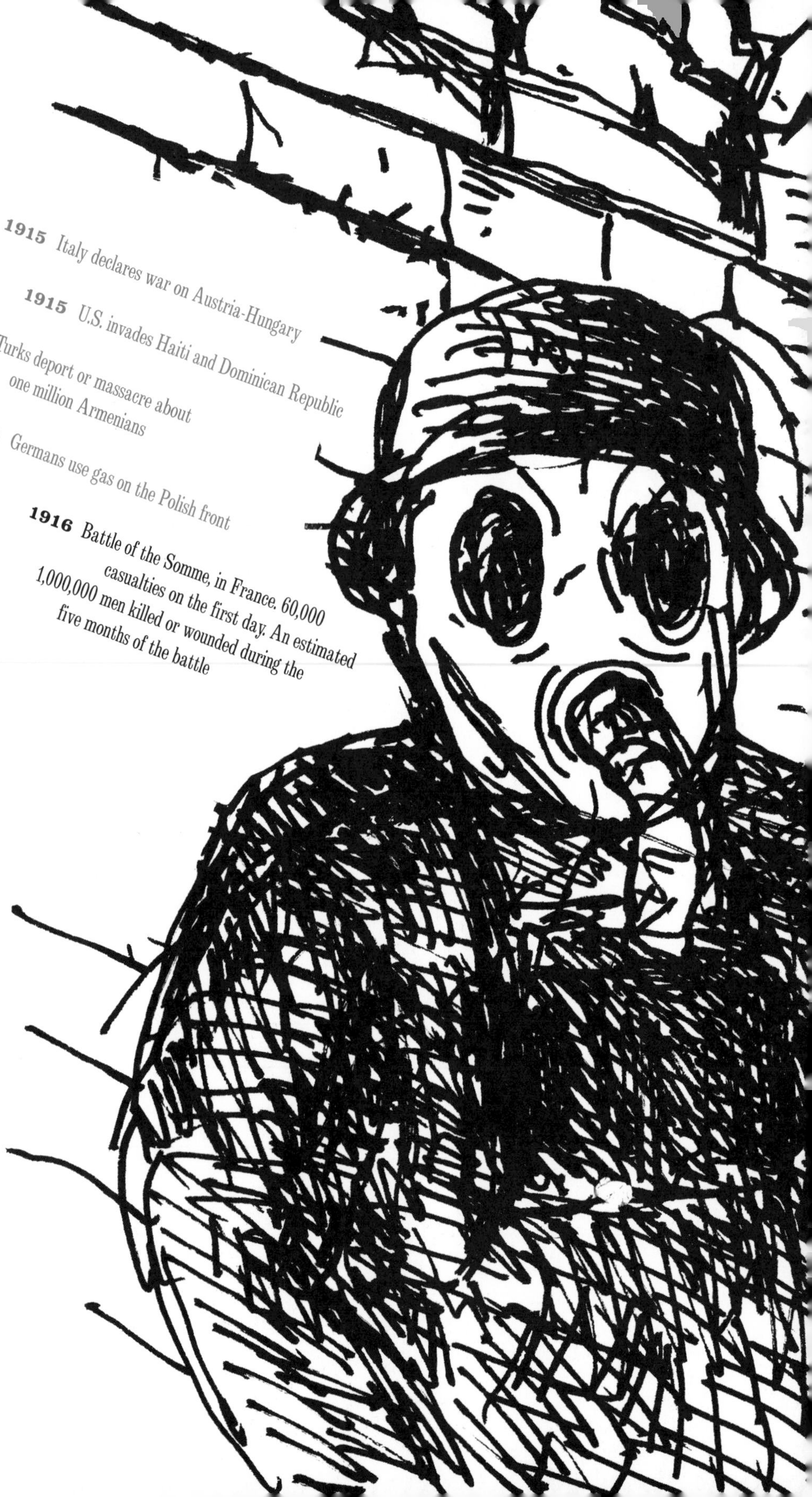

1915 Italy declares war on Austria-Hungary

1915 U.S. invades Haiti and Dominican Republic

1915 Turks deport or massacre about one million Armenians

1915 Germans use gas on the Polish front

1916 Battle of the Somme, in France. 60,000 casualties on the first day. An estimated 1,000,000 men killed or wounded during the five months of the battle

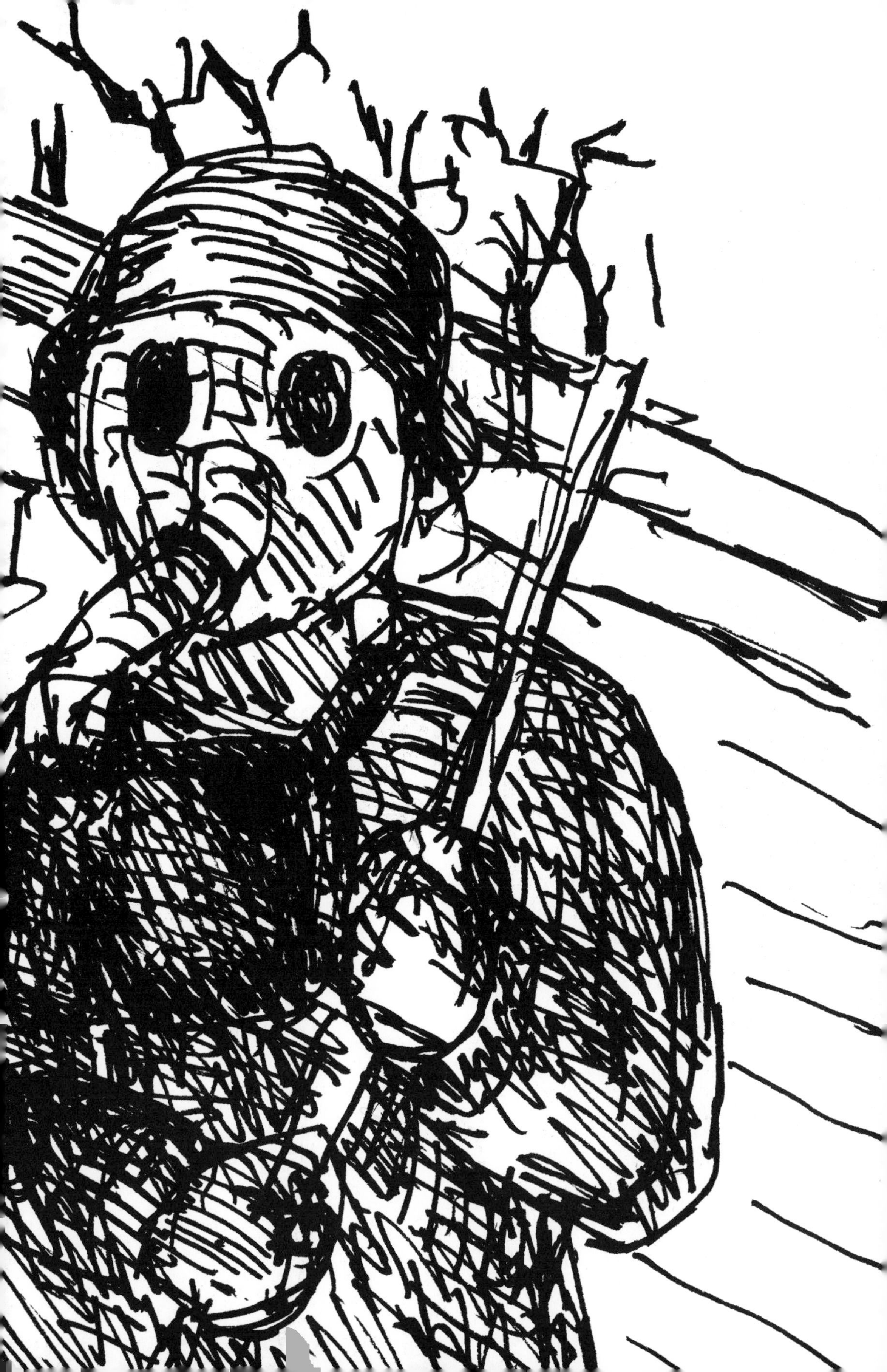

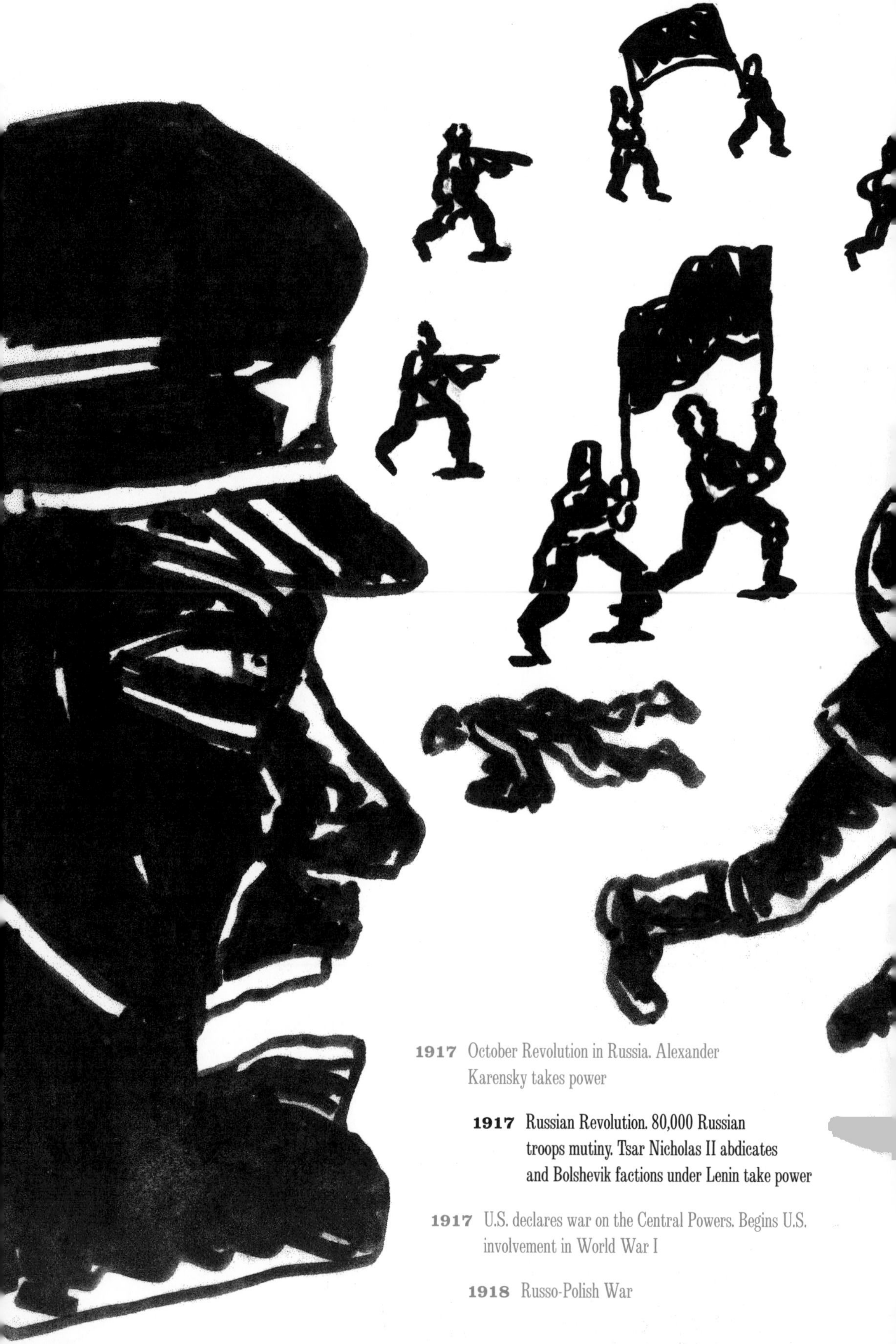

1917 October Revolution in Russia. Alexander Karensky takes power

1917 Russian Revolution. 80,000 Russian troops mutiny. Tsar Nicholas II abdicates and Bolshevik factions under Lenin take power

1917 U.S. declares war on the Central Powers. Begins U.S. involvement in World War I

1918 Russo-Polish War

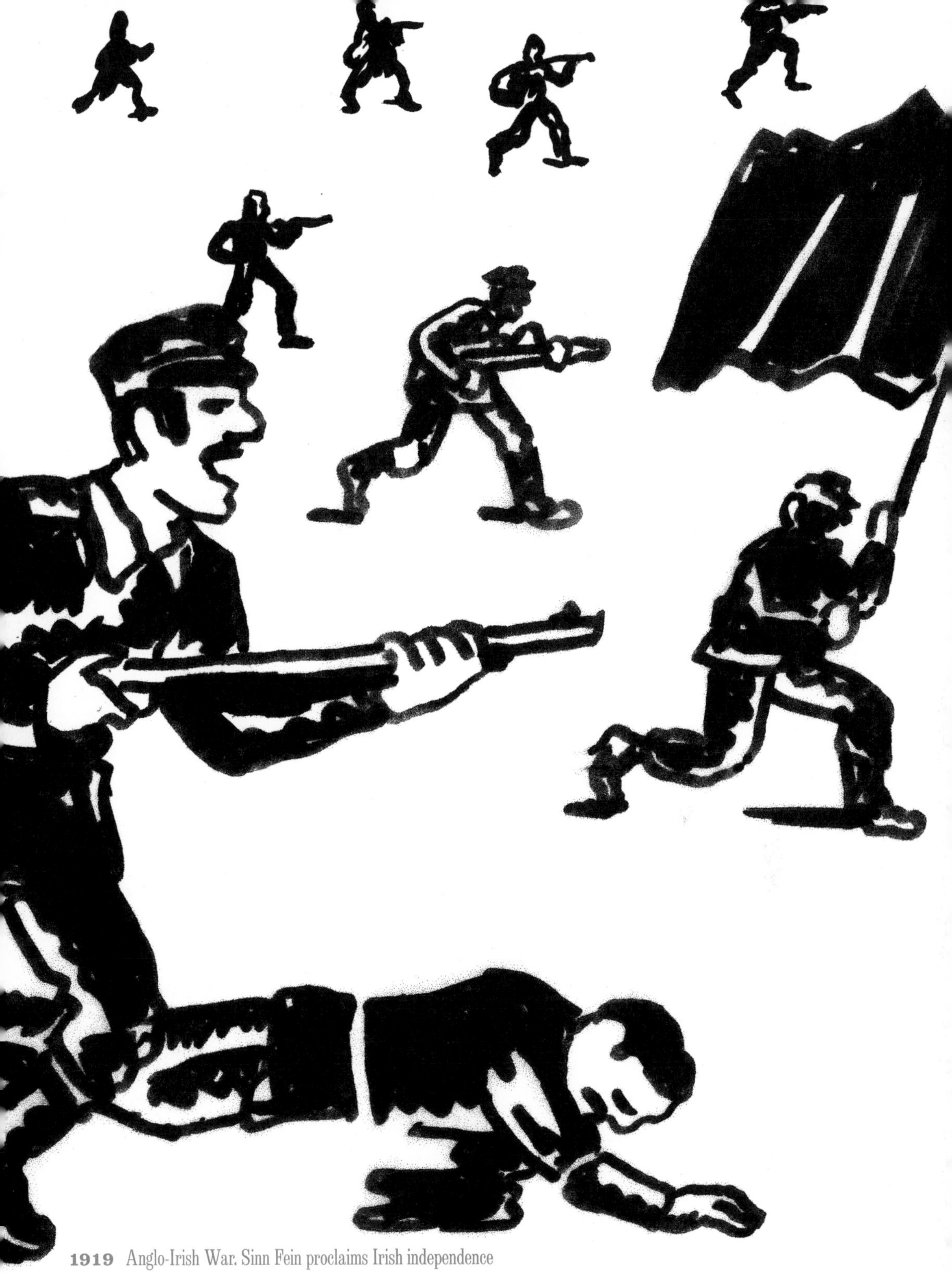

1919 Anglo-Irish War. Sinn Fein proclaims Irish independence

1921 Morocco defeats Spain at the Battle of Annual

1922 Turks defeat Greeks in Asia Minor

1921 Greeks make war with Turks

1925 Civil War in China. Chiang Kai-shek gains power

1926 U.S. occupies Nicaragua

1927 France launches major campaign against Druze uprising in Syria

1930 Military revolution in Brazil

1931 Japan invades and occupies Manchuria

1936 Germany supports Fascists fighting Republicans in the Spanish Civil War

1939 General Franco captures Madrid, ending the Spanish Civil War

1939 Germans invade Poland. Anglo-French declaration of war prompts World War II

1940 Germans invade France, Belgium, Luxemburg and the Netherlands

1940 Japan joins Germany and Italy in World War II

1940 Fall of France to Germans

1941 Japan begins control of southeast Asia

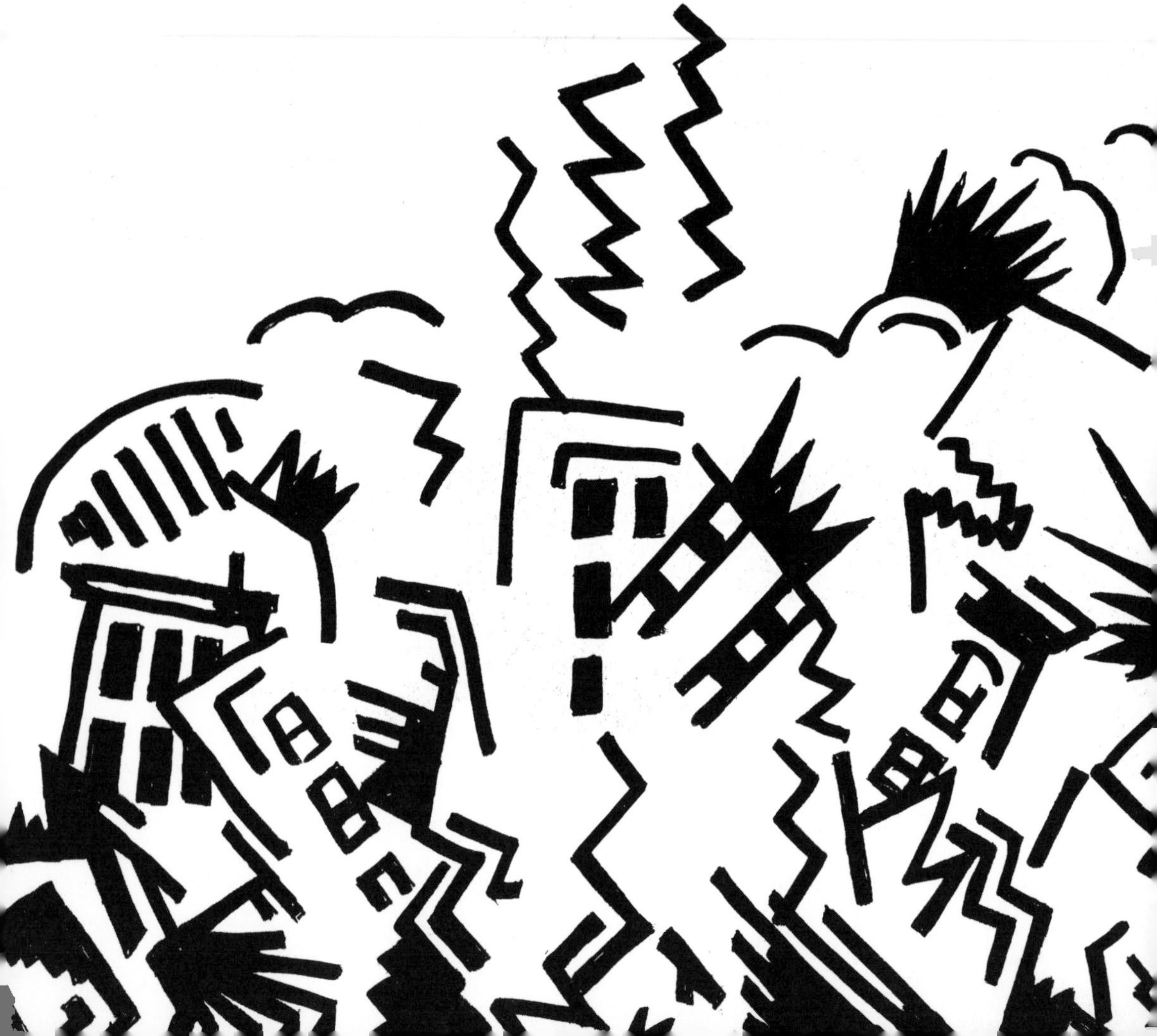

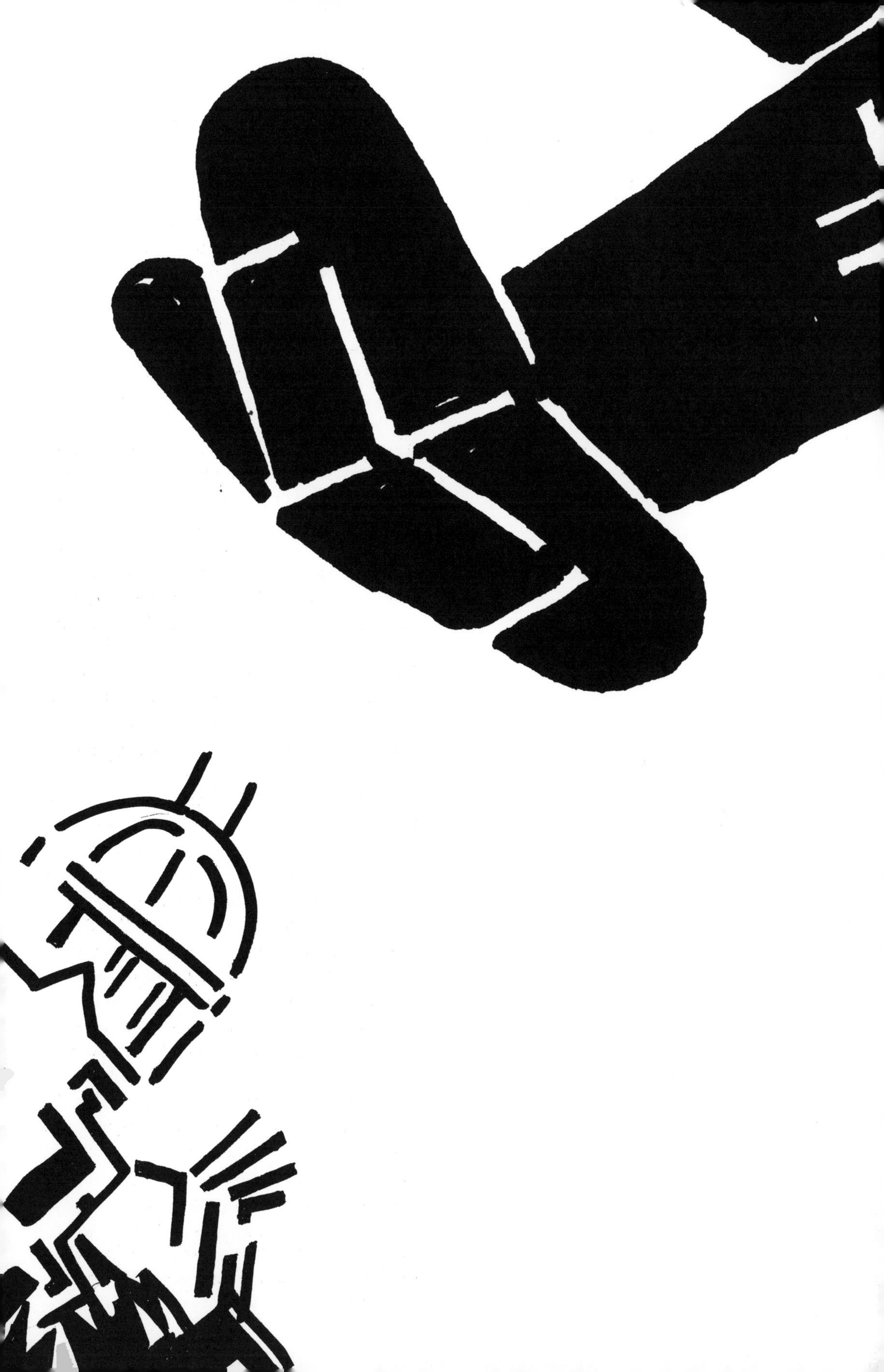

Randolph Bourne

War is the Health of the State

This excerpt is from the 1918 essay "The State."

The State is the country acting as a political unit, it is the group acting as a repository of force, determiner of law, arbiter of justice. International politics is a "power politics" because it is a relation of States and that is what States infallibly and calamitously are, huge aggregations of human and industrial force that may be hurled against each other in war. When a country acts as a whole in relation to another country, or in imposing laws on its own inhabitants, or in coercing or punishing individuals or minorities, it is acting as a State. The history of America as a country is quite different from that of America as a State. In one case it is the drama of the pioneering conquest of the land, of the growth of wealth and the ways in which it was used, of the enterprise of education, and the carrying out of spiritual ideals, of the struggle of economic classes. But as a State, its history is that of playing a part in the world, making war, obstructing international trade, preventing itself from being split to pieces, punishing those citizens whom society agrees are offensive and collecting money to pay...

There is, of course, in the feeling toward the State a large element of pure filial mysticism. The sense of insecurity, the desire for protection, sends one's desire back to the father and mother, with whom is associated the earliest feelings of protection. It is not for nothing that one's State is still thought of as Father or Motherland, that one's relation toward it is conceived in terms of family affection. The war has shown that nowhere under the shock of danger have these primitive childlike attitudes failed to assert themselves again, as much in this country as anywhere. If we have not the intense Father-sense of the German who worships his Vaterland, at least in Uncle Sam we have a symbol of protecting, kindly authority, and in the many Mother-posters of the Red Cross, we see how easily in the more tender functions of war service, the ruling organization is conceived in family terms. A people at war have become in the most literal sense obedient, respectful, trustful children again, full of that naïve faith in the all-wisdom and all-power of the adult who takes care of them, imposes his mild but necessary rule upon them and in whom they lose their responsibility and anxieties. In this recrudescence of the child, there is great comfort, and a certain influx of power. On most people the strain of being an independent adult weighs heavily, and upon none more than those members of the significant classes who have had bequeathed to them or have assumed the responsibilities of governing. The State provides the convenientest of symbols under which these classes can retain all the actual pragmatic satisfaction of governing, but can rid themselves of the psychic burden of adulthood. They continue to direct industry and government and all the institutions of society pretty much as before, but in their own conscious eyes and in the eyes of the general public, they are turned from their selfish and predatory ways, and have become loyal servants of society, or something greater than they—the

State. The man who moves from the direction of a large business in New York to a post in the war management industrial service in Washington does not apparently alter very much his power or his administrative technique. But psychically, what a transfiguration has occurred! His is now not only the power but the glory! And his sense of satisfaction is directly proportional not to the genuine amount of personal sacrifice that may be involved in the change but to the extent to which he retains his industrial prerogatives and sense of command...

Wartime brings the ideal of the State out into very clear relief, and reveals attitudes and tendencies that were hidden. In times of peace the sense of the State flags in a republic that is not militarized. For war is essentially the health of the State. The ideal of the State is that within its territory its power and influence should be universal. As the Church is the medium for the spiritual salvation of man, so the State is thought of as the medium for his political salvation. Its idealism is a rich blood flowing to all the members of the body politic. And it is precisely in war that the urgency for union seems greatest, and the necessity for universality seems most unquestioned. The State is the organization of the herd to act offensively or defensively against another herd similarly organized. The more terrifying the occasion for defense, the closer will become the organization and the more coercive the influence upon each member of the herd. War sends the current of purpose and activity flowing down to the lowest level of the herd, and to its most remote branches. All the activities of society are linked together as fast as possible to this central purpose of making a military offensive or a military defense, and the State becomes what in peacetimes it has vainly struggled to become — the inexorable arbiter and determinant of men's business and attitudes and opinions. The slack is taken up, the cross-currents fade out and the nation moves lumberingly and slowly, but with ever accelerated speed and integration, toward the great end, toward the "peacefulness of being at war," of which L.P. Jacks has so unforgettably spoken.

The classes which are able to play an active and not merely a passive role in the organization for war get a tremendous liberation of activity and energy. Individuals are jolted out of their old routine, many of them are given new positions of responsibility, new techniques must be learned. Wearing home ties are broken and women who would have remained attached with infantile bonds are liberated for service overseas. A vast sense of rejuvenescence pervades the significant classes, a sense of new importance in the world. Old national ideals are taken out, re-adapted to the purpose and used as universal touchstones, or molds into which all thought is poured. Every individual citizen who in peacetimes had no function to perform by which he could imagine himself an expression or living fragment of the State becomes an active amateur agent of the Government in reporting spies and disloyalists, in raising Government funds or in propagating such measures as are considered necessary by officialdom. Minority opinion, which in times of peace, was only irritating and could not be dealt with by law unless it was conjoined with actual crime, becomes, with the outbreak of war, a case for outlawry. Criticism of the State, objections to war, lukewarm opinions concerning the necessity or the beauty of conscription, are made subject to ferocious penalties, far exceeding in severity those affixed to actual pragmatic crimes. Public opinion, as expressed in the newspapers, and the pulpits and the schools, becomes one solid block. "Loyalty," or rather war orthodoxy, becomes the sole test for all professions, techniques, occupations. Particularly is this true in the sphere of the intellectual life. There the smallest taint is held to spread over the whole soul, so that a professor of physics is ipso facto disqualified to teach physics or to hold honorable place in a university — the republic of learning — if he is at all unsound on the war. Even mere association with persons thus tainted is considered to disqualify a teacher. Anything pertaining to the enemy becomes taboo. His books are suppressed wherever possible, his language is forbidden. His artistic products are considered to convey in the subtlest spiritual way taints of vast poison to the soul that permits itself to enjoy them. So enemy music is suppressed, and energetic measures of opprobrium taken against those whose artistic consciences are not ready to perform such an act of self-sacrifice. The rage for loyal conformity works impartially, and often in diametric opposition to other orthodoxies and traditional conformities, or even ideals. The triumphant orthodoxy of the State is shown at its apex perhaps when Christian preachers lose their pulpits for taking in more or less literal terms the Sermon on the Mount, and Christian zealots are sent to prison for twenty years for distributing tracts which argue that war is unscriptural.

War is the health of the State. It automatically sets in motion throughout society those irresistible forces for uniformity, for passionate cooperation with the Government in coercing into obedience the minority groups and individuals which lack the larger herd sense. The machinery of government sets and enforces the drastic penalties; the minorities are either intimidated into silence, or brought slowly around by a subtle process of persuasion which may seem to them really to be converting them. Of course, the ideal of perfect loyalty, perfect uniformity is never really attained. The classes upon whom the amateur work of coercion falls are unwearied in their zeal, but often their agitation instead of converting, merely serves to stiffen their resistance. Minorities are rendered sullen, and some intellectual opinion bitter and satirical. But in general, the nation in wartime attains a uniformity of feeling, a hierarchy of values culminating at the undisputed apex of the State ideal, which could not possibly be produced through any other agency than war.

1941 Japanese attack on Pearl Harbor. U.S. declares war

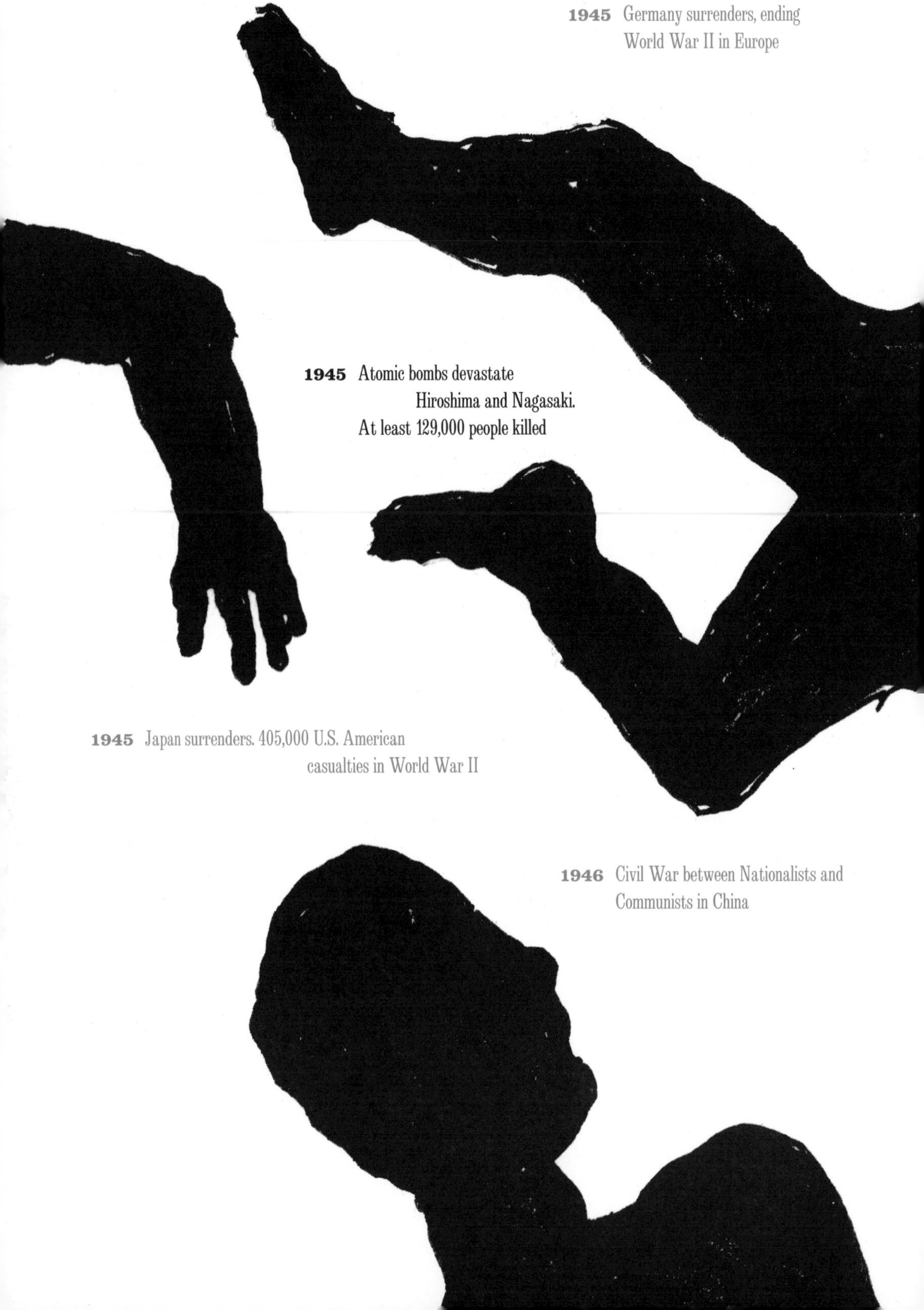

1945 Germany surrenders, ending World War II in Europe

1945 Atomic bombs devastate Hiroshima and Nagasaki. At least 129,000 people killed

1945 Japan surrenders. 405,000 U.S. American casualties in World War II

1946 Civil War between Nationalists and Communists in China

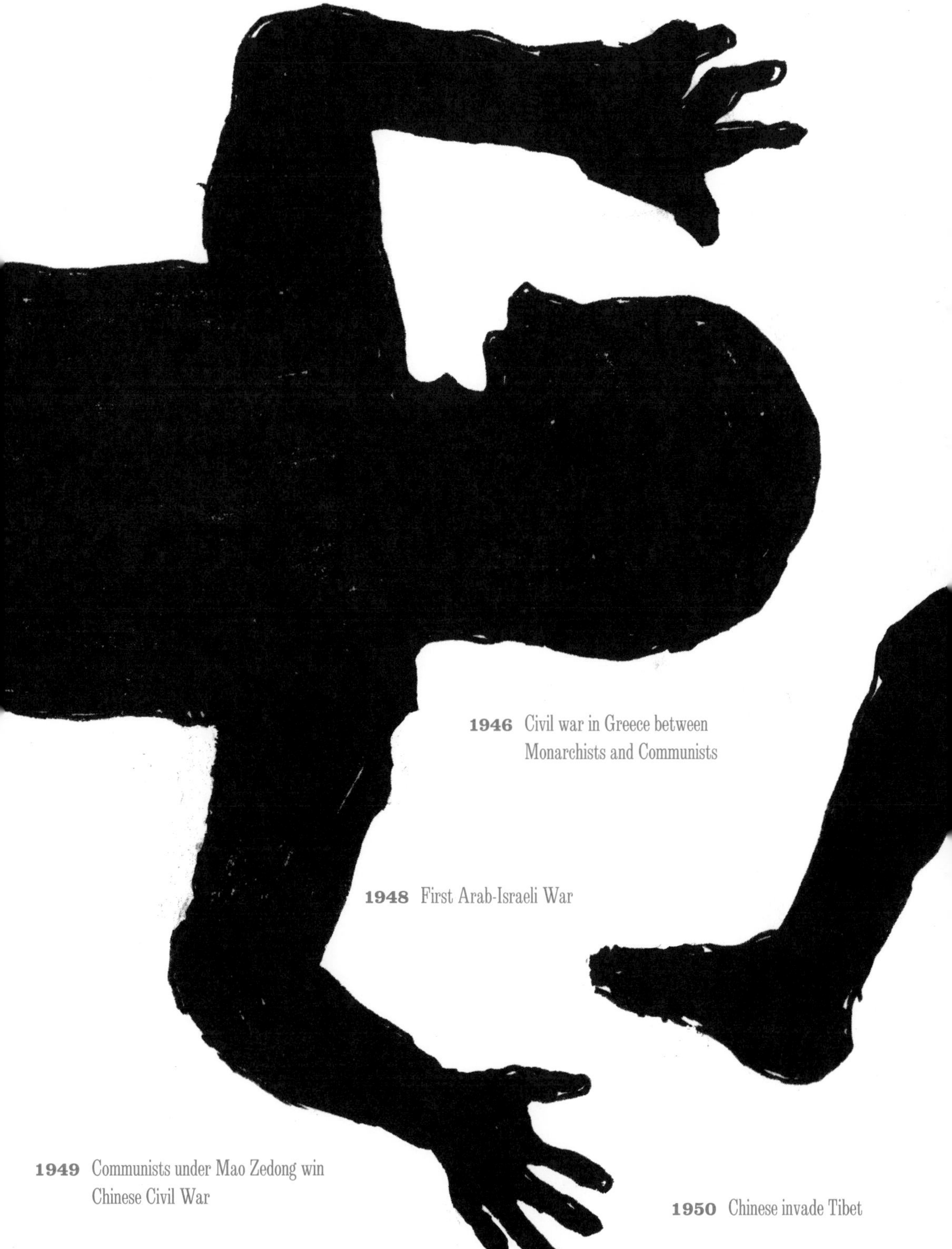

1946 France fights Ho Chi Minh in Indochina

1946 Civil war in Greece between Monarchists and Communists

1948 First Arab-Israeli War

1949 Communists under Mao Zedong win Chinese Civil War

1950 Chinese invade Tibet

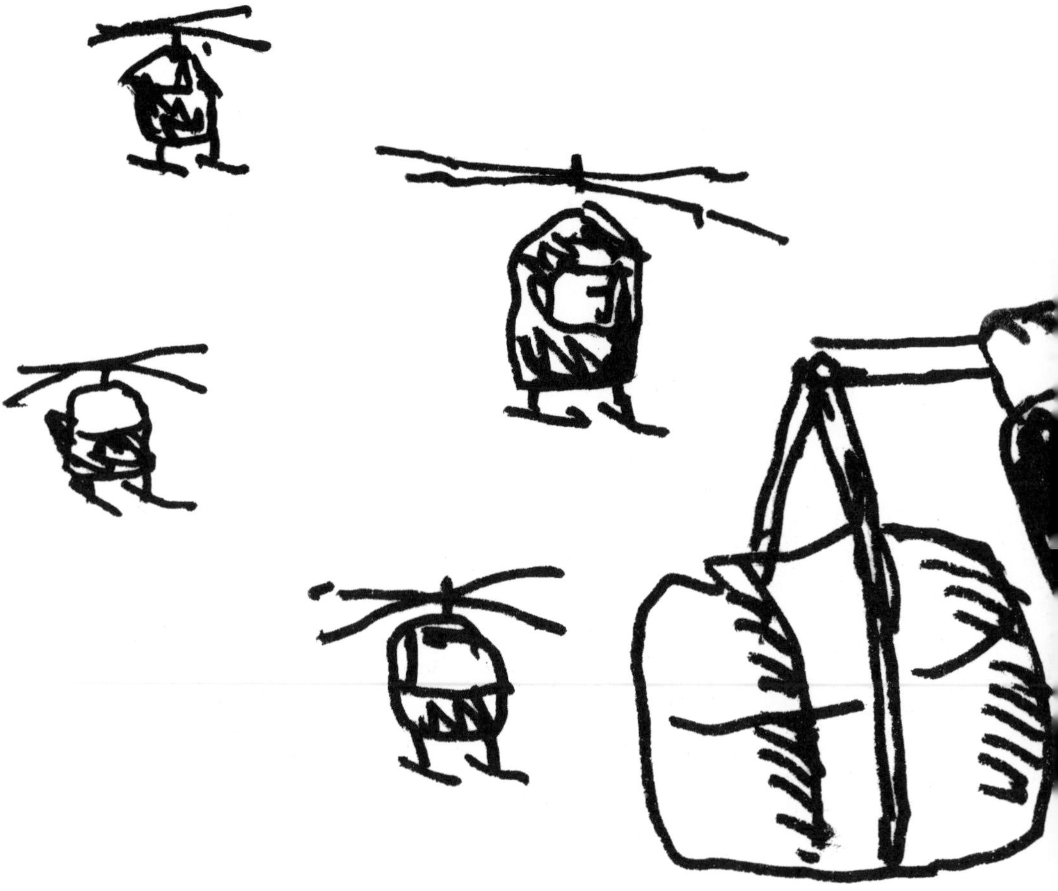

1950 North and South Korea at war; U.S. and China join in

1952 Mau Mau Rebellion in Kenya

1954 French defeated at Diem Bien Phu. Vietnam is divided

1954 Algerian War of Independence against France

1956 French and English take Egypt's Suez Canal

1957 South Vietnam attacked by Viet Cong

1959 Fidel Castro leads Communists to power in Cuba

1960 War between Communists and non-Communists in Vietnam

1964 Beginning of Vietnam War. 58,000 Americans die; 75,000 severely disabled. Estimates of Vietnamese killed: 800,000 to 3.1 million

1967 Six-Day War. Arab forces attack Israel and are defeated

1968 Warsaw Pact invasion of Czechoslovakia

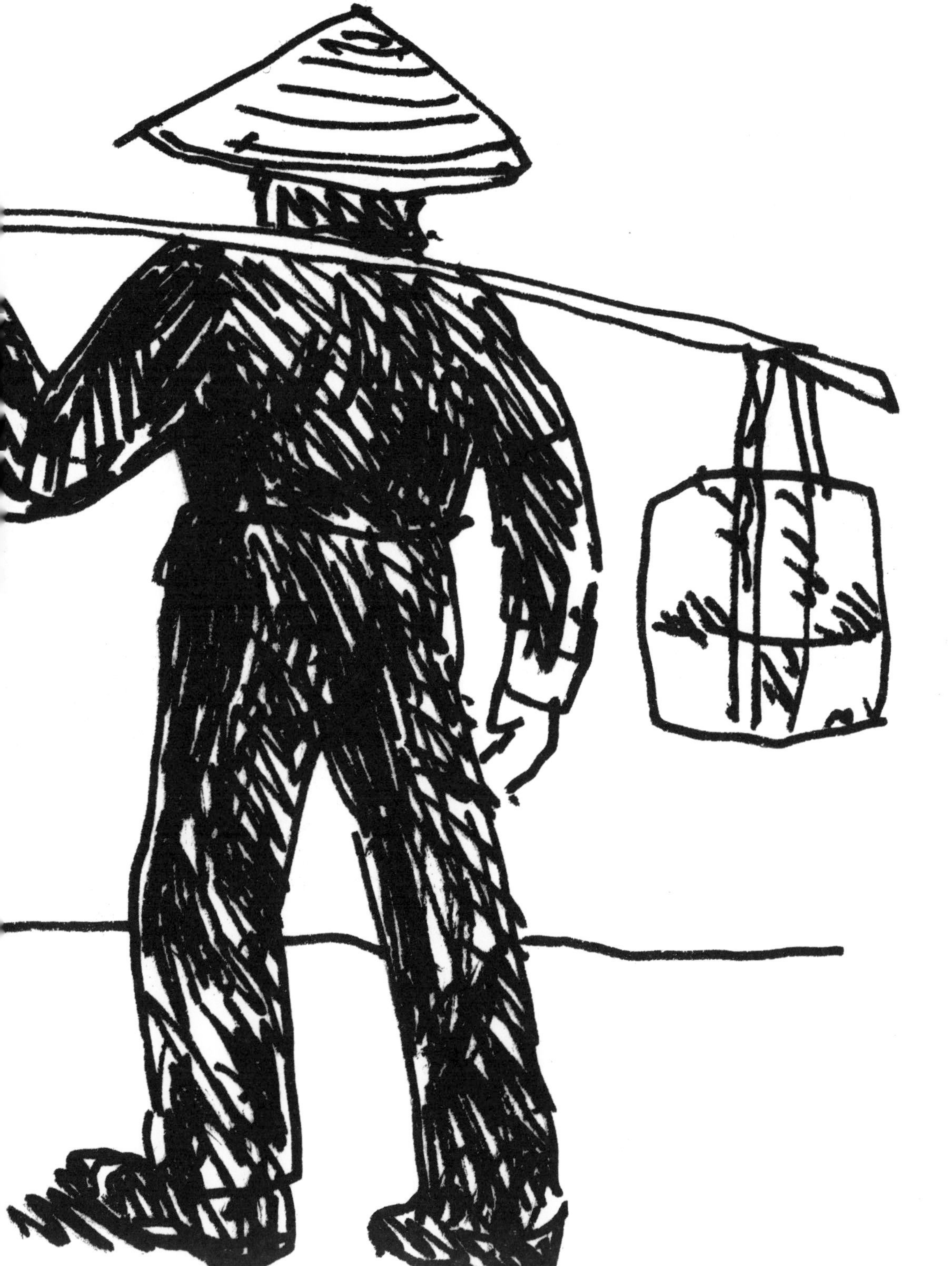

1971 East Pakistan becomes Bangladesh with a civil war

1971 Idi Amin seizes power in Uganda. 100,000 to 500,000 people killed
His aggression leads to Uganda-Tanzania War

1975 Kmer Rouge's Pol Pot seizes control of Cambodia. 200,000 to 300,000 killed

1977 Cambodia-Vietnam War

1978 Ugandan Civil War

1979 USSR invades Afghanistan

1979 Civil War in Nicaragua. Sandinistas vs. Contras

1980 Iran-Iraq War

1982 Israel invades Lebanon

1982 Falkland War between Argentina and U.K.

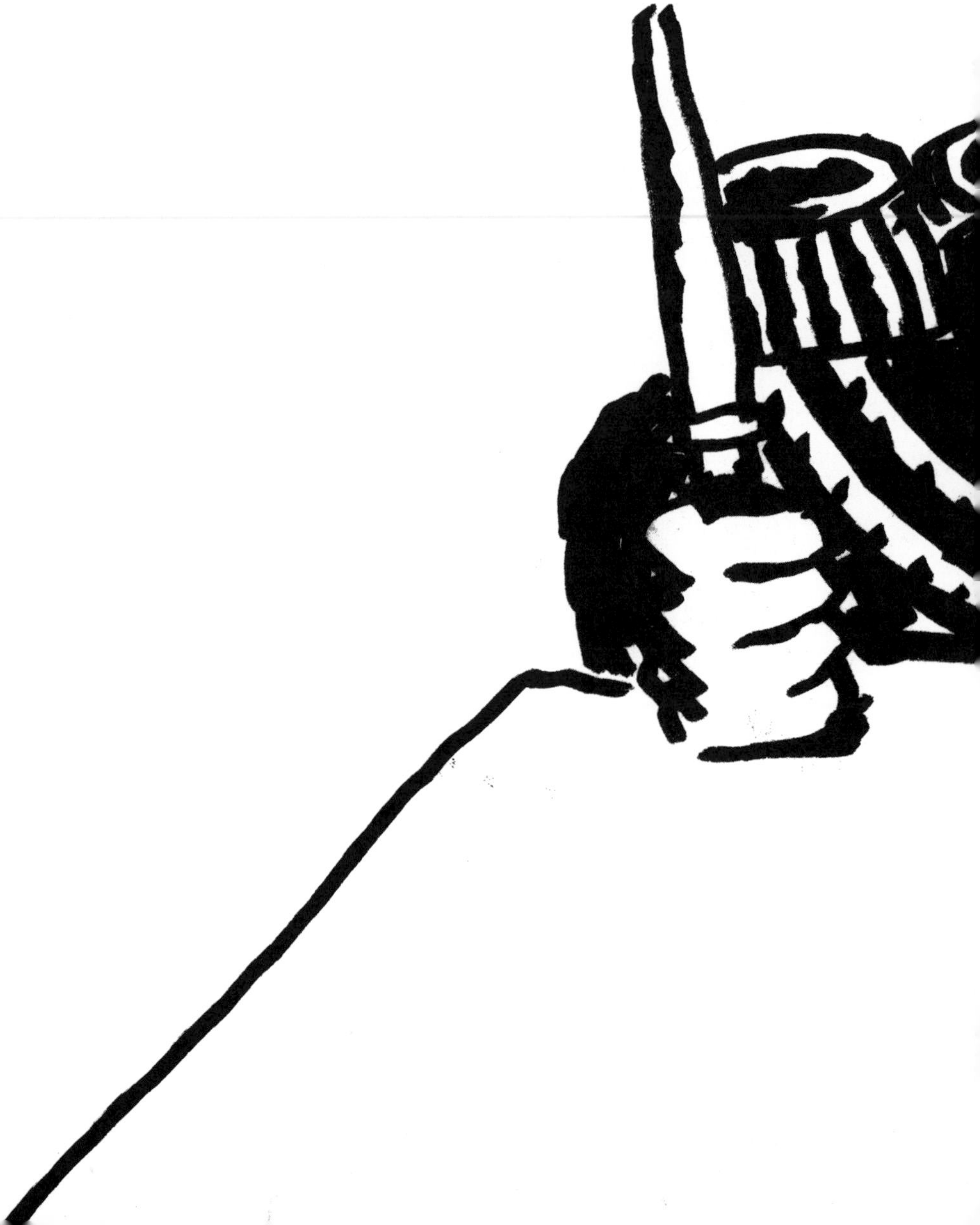

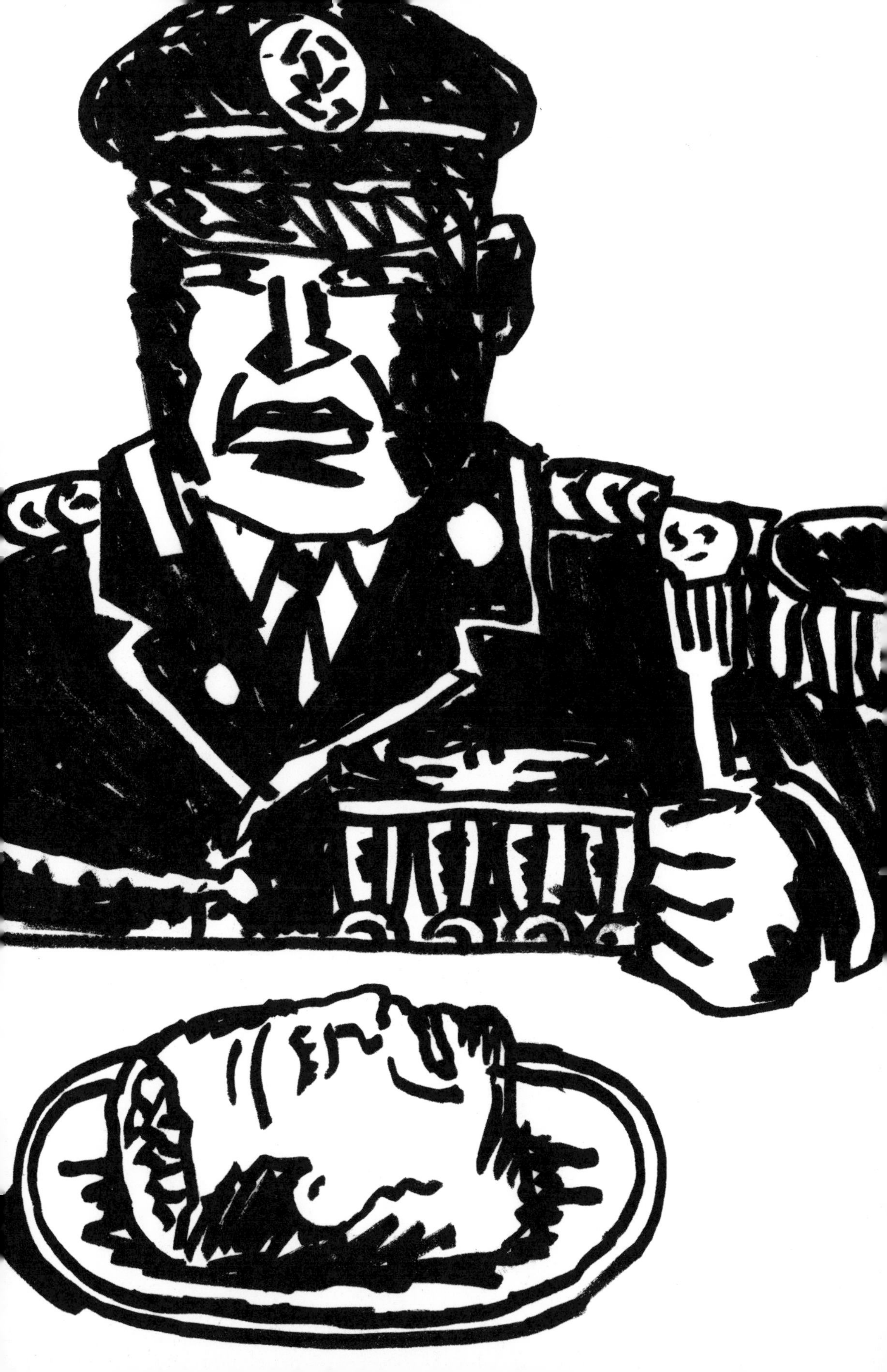

1983 Tamil Tigers fight guerrilla war against Sri Lanka government

1983 U.S. invades Granada in a military intervention

1989 Over 600,000 people killed in the First Liberian Civil War

1990 Iraq's Saddam Hussein invades Kuwait

1991 U.N. ends 10-year civil war in El Salvador

1991 Gulf War. U.S. launches battle against Iraqi forces who lose an estimated 200,000 lives

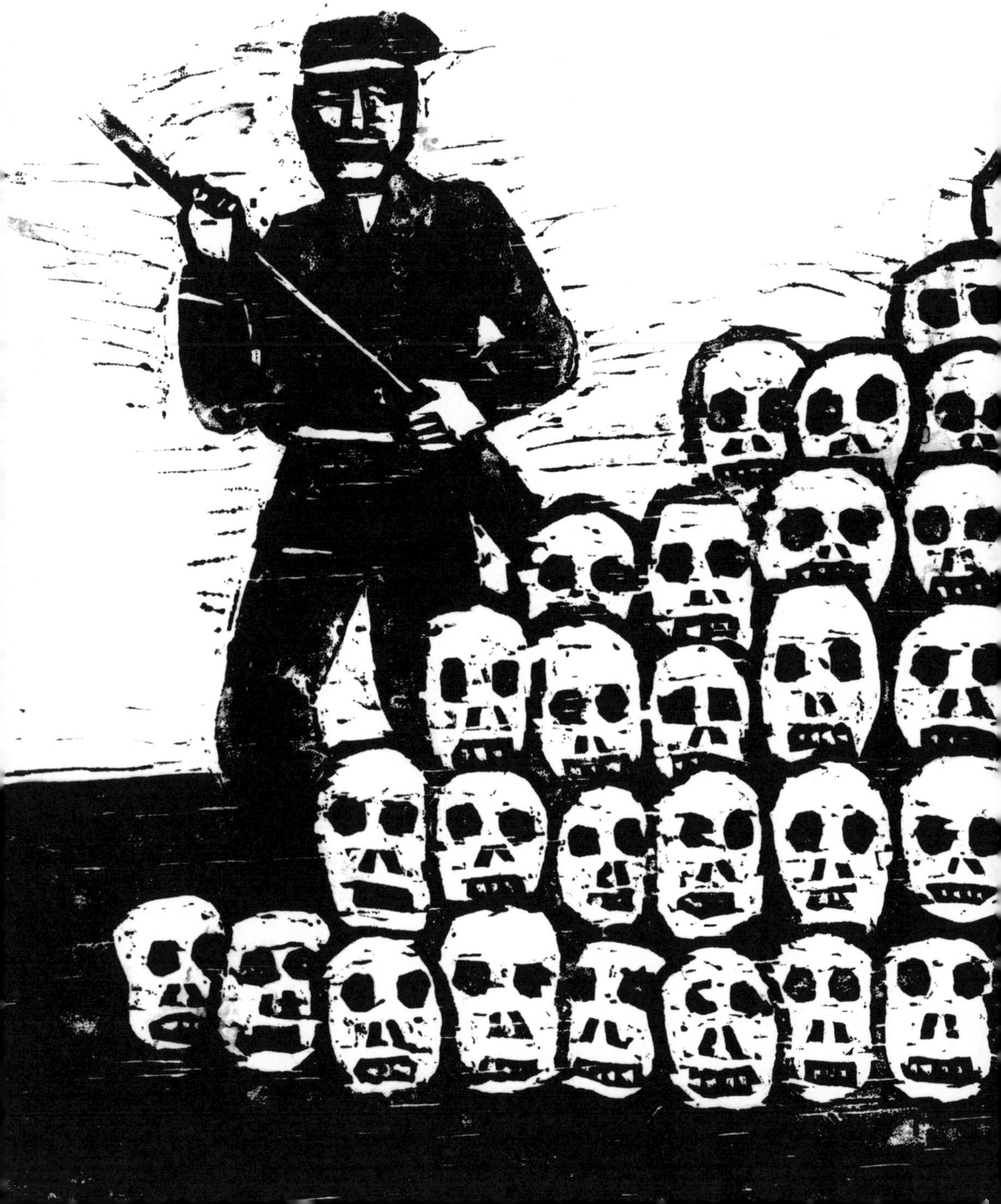

1992 Bosnia-Herzegovina, three-year war between Muslims, Serbs and Croats

1992 U.S. and U.N. intervene to end famine and civil war in Somalia

1994 War between Christian Armenia and Muslim Azerbaijan

1994 Tutsis massacred by Hutus in Rwanda's civil war where 500,000 to 1,000,000 Rwandans are killed. Perpetrators include the Hutu civilian population

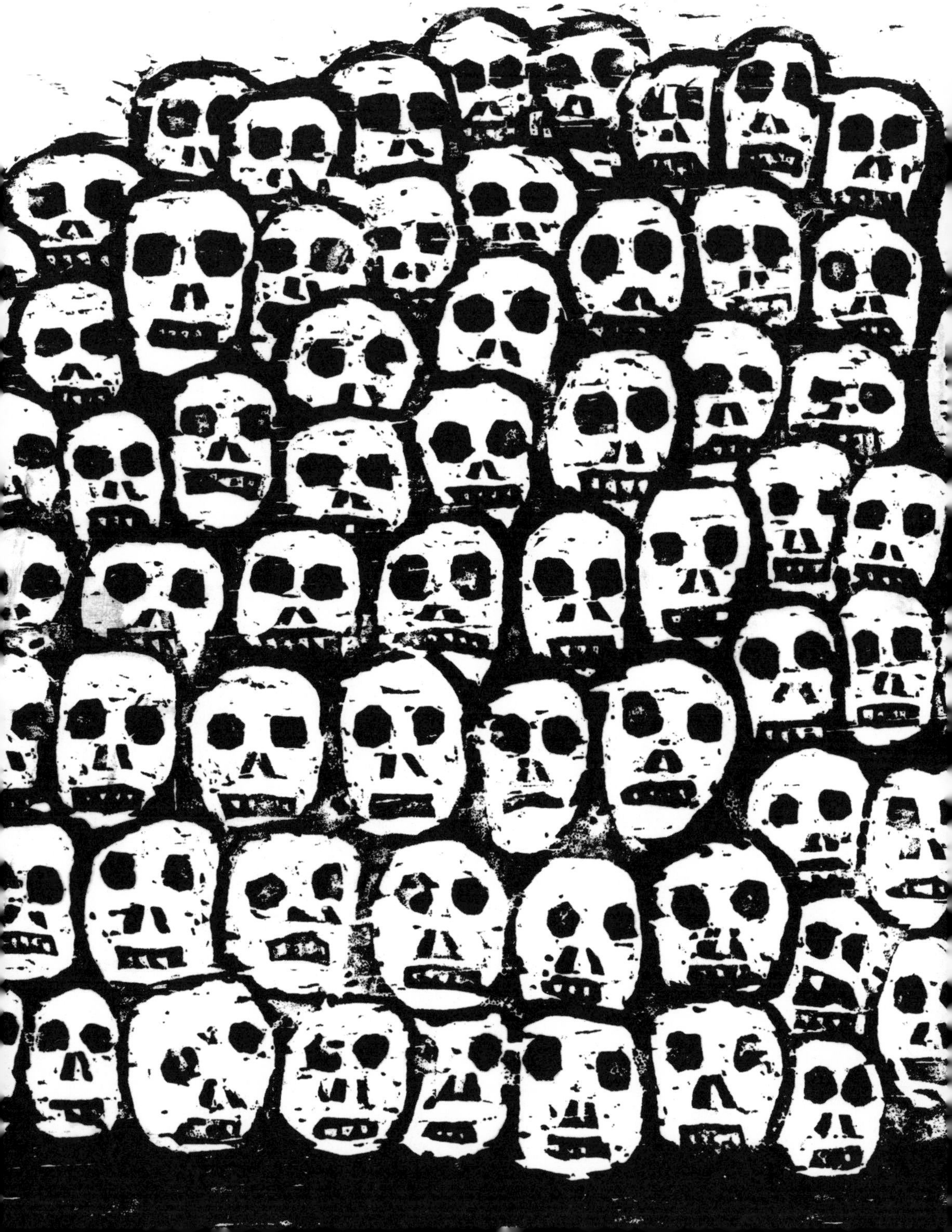

1994 First Chechen War with Russia

1994 Zapatista Rebellion in Mexico

1996 First Congo War. Rwanda conquers Zaire, renamed the Democratic Republic of the Congo. Leads to Second Congo War

1996 Taliban captures Kabul and declares Islamic State of Afghanistan

1998 Bombing attacks at U.S. embassies in Nairobi and other cities by Al-Qaida

1998 Oklahoma City's Federal Building bombed, killing 250 people

1998 Serbs attack Kosovo Albanian civilians. U.S. brokers a cease-fire

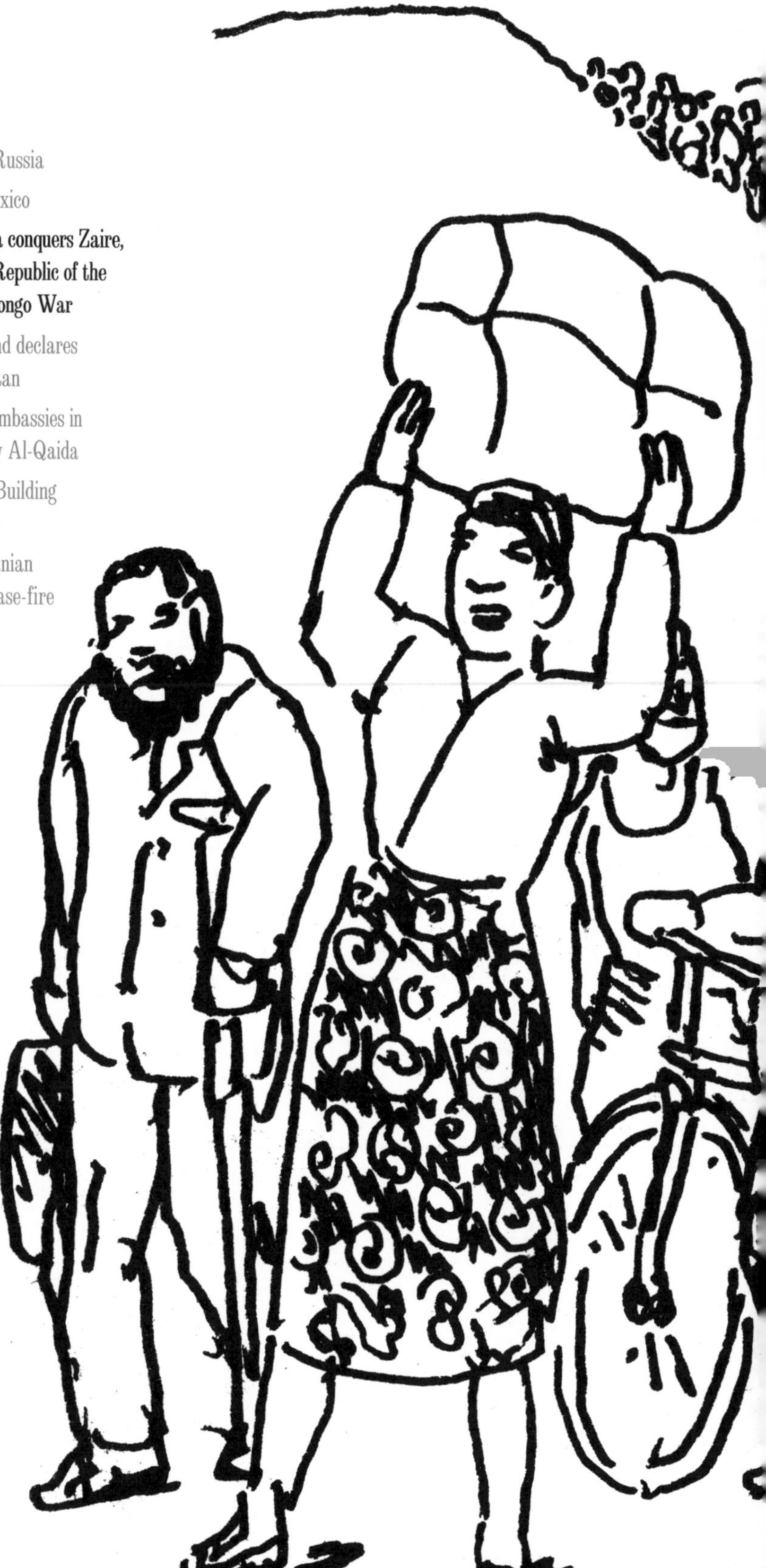

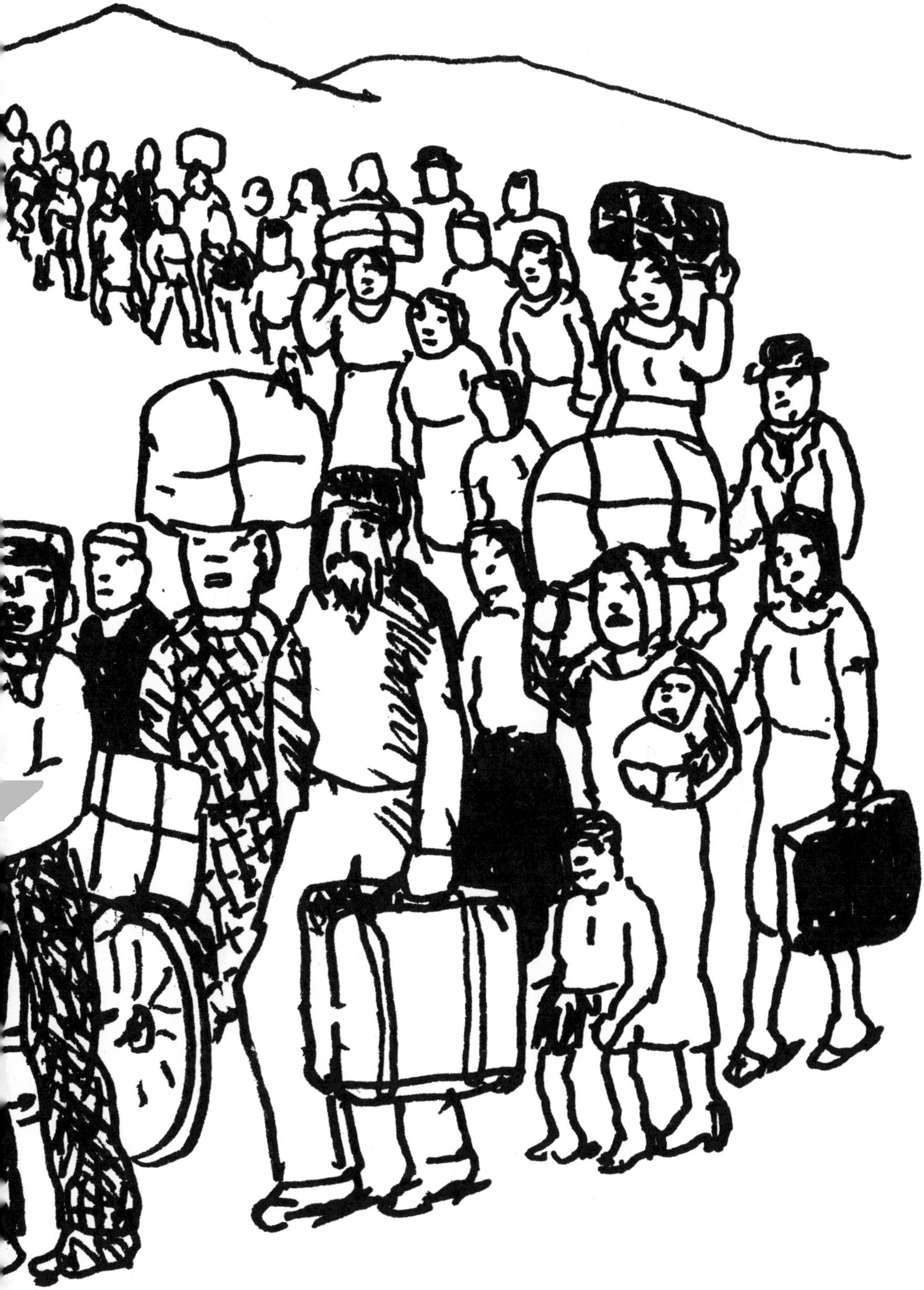

1999 NATO troops sent to maintain peace in Kosovo

1999 Second Chechen War

2001 More than 3000 dead when Osama bin Laden's terrorists crash airliners into World Trade Center

2002 U.S. attacks Al-Qaida forces in Afghanistan

2002 Hindu majority and Muslim minority attack each other in India. Hundreds killed

2003 Liberia's Charles Taylor defeated during Second Liberian Civil War

2003 Soldiers from U.S., U.K., Australia and Poland invade Iraq looking for nonexistent weapons of mass destruction. 3000 U.S. soldiers dead. 55,000 civilians killed

2004 Spain is rocked by terrorist attacks. Over 200 dead

2004 Chechen terrorists take 1200 schoolchildren hostage

2004 Pakistan's A.Q. Khan sells nuclear-weapons designs to North Korea, Iran and Libya

2005 London hit by terrorist bombings killing 52 and wounding 700

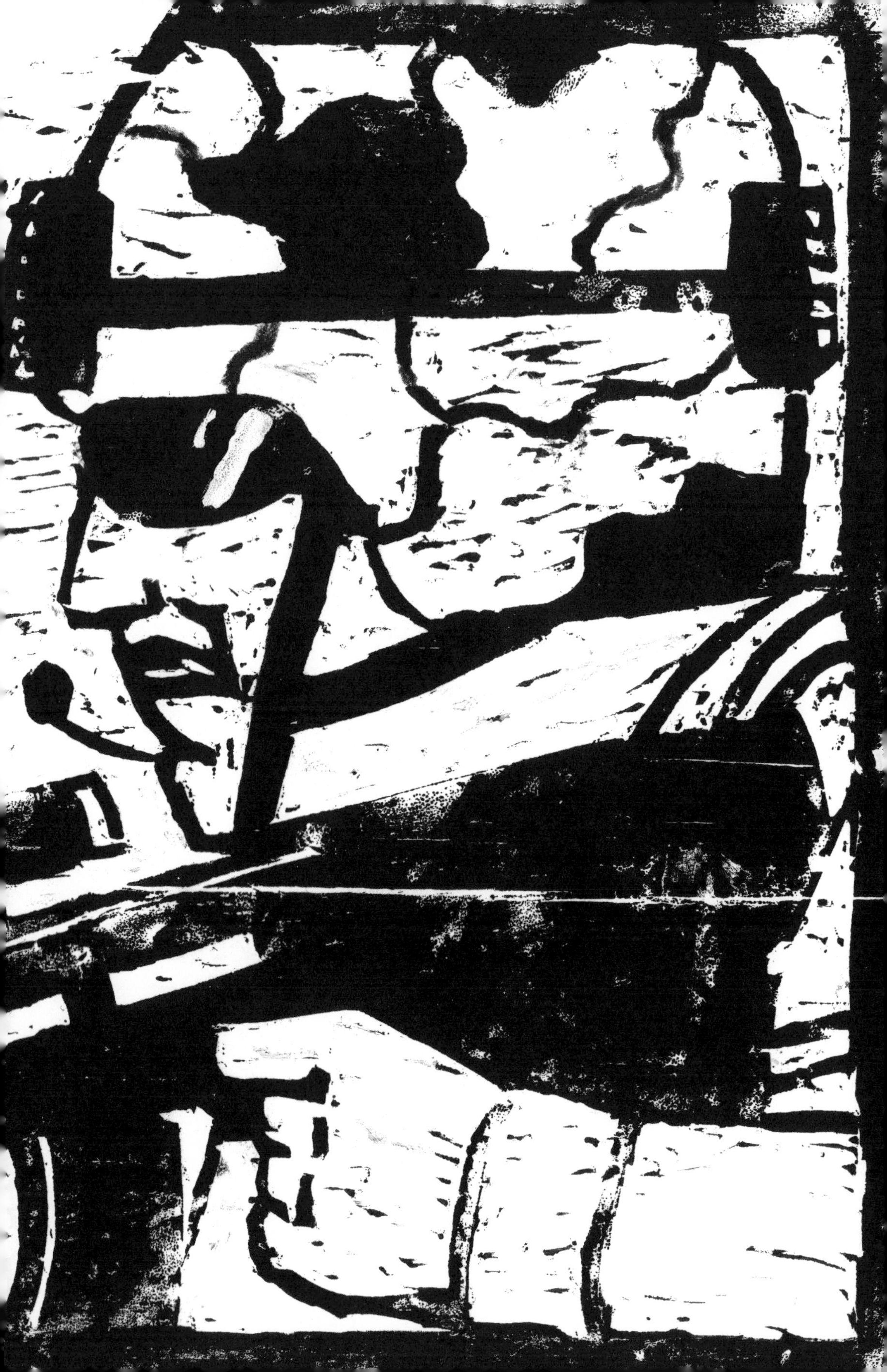

2006 Bombs explode on commuter trains in Mumbai. Over 200 people dead

2013 South Sudanese Civil War (ongoing)

2013 Russians kill Islamist rebels in Chechnya

2014 Israel launches ground offensive into Gaza in July and August. 2143 Palestinians and 64 Israeli soldiers killed.

2014 In Ukraine armed conflict between Russian and separatist forces and the Ukrainian government

2015 Heavy fighting between Somali forces, Al-Qaida militants and Al-Shabaab militants

2015 Central African Republic: Seleka and rebel groups clash in Markounda

2015 **In Syria and Iraq U.S. trained rebels fight with ISIL, Islamic State and the Levant, a jihadist fundamentalist group. Ongoing**

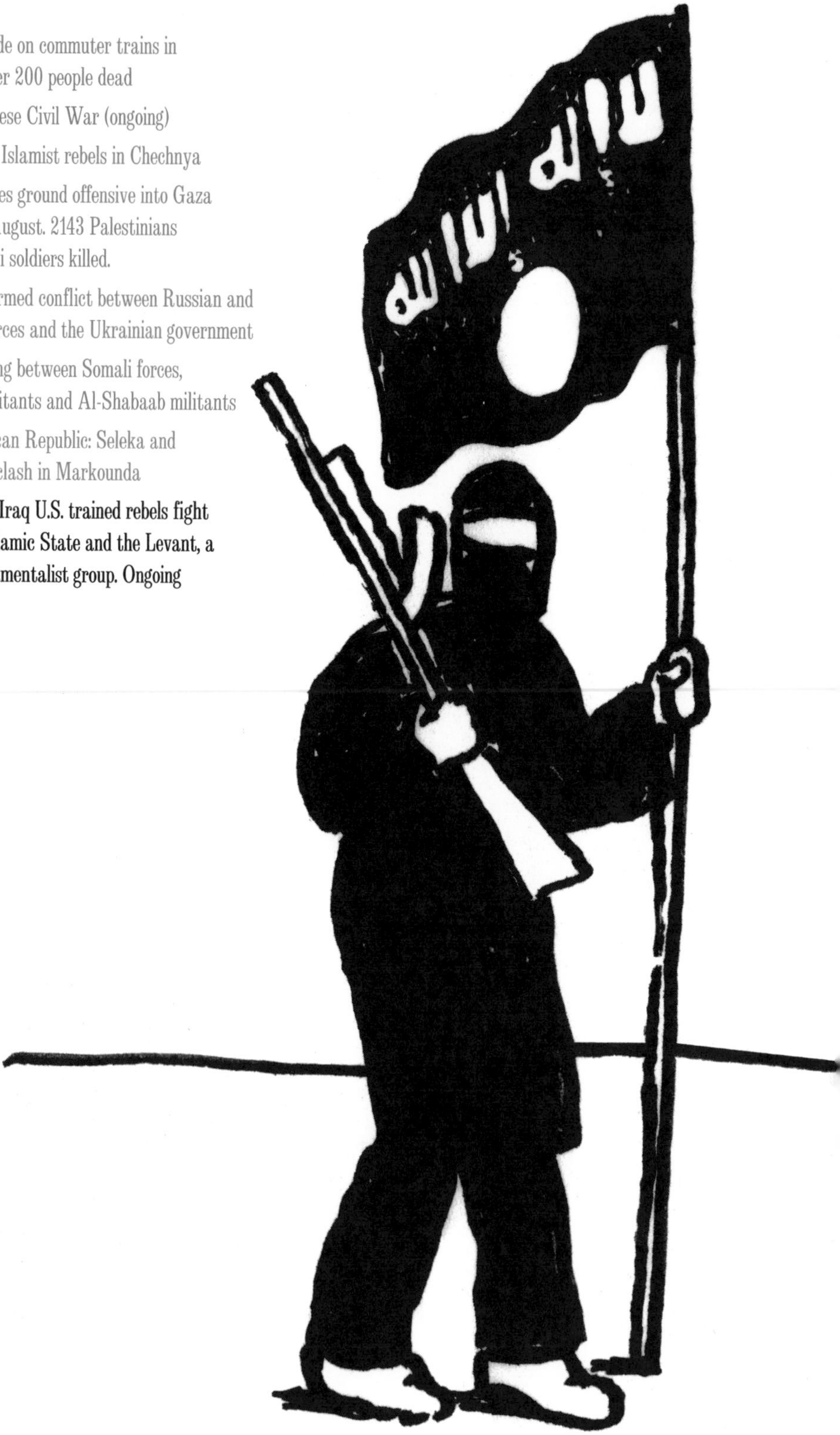

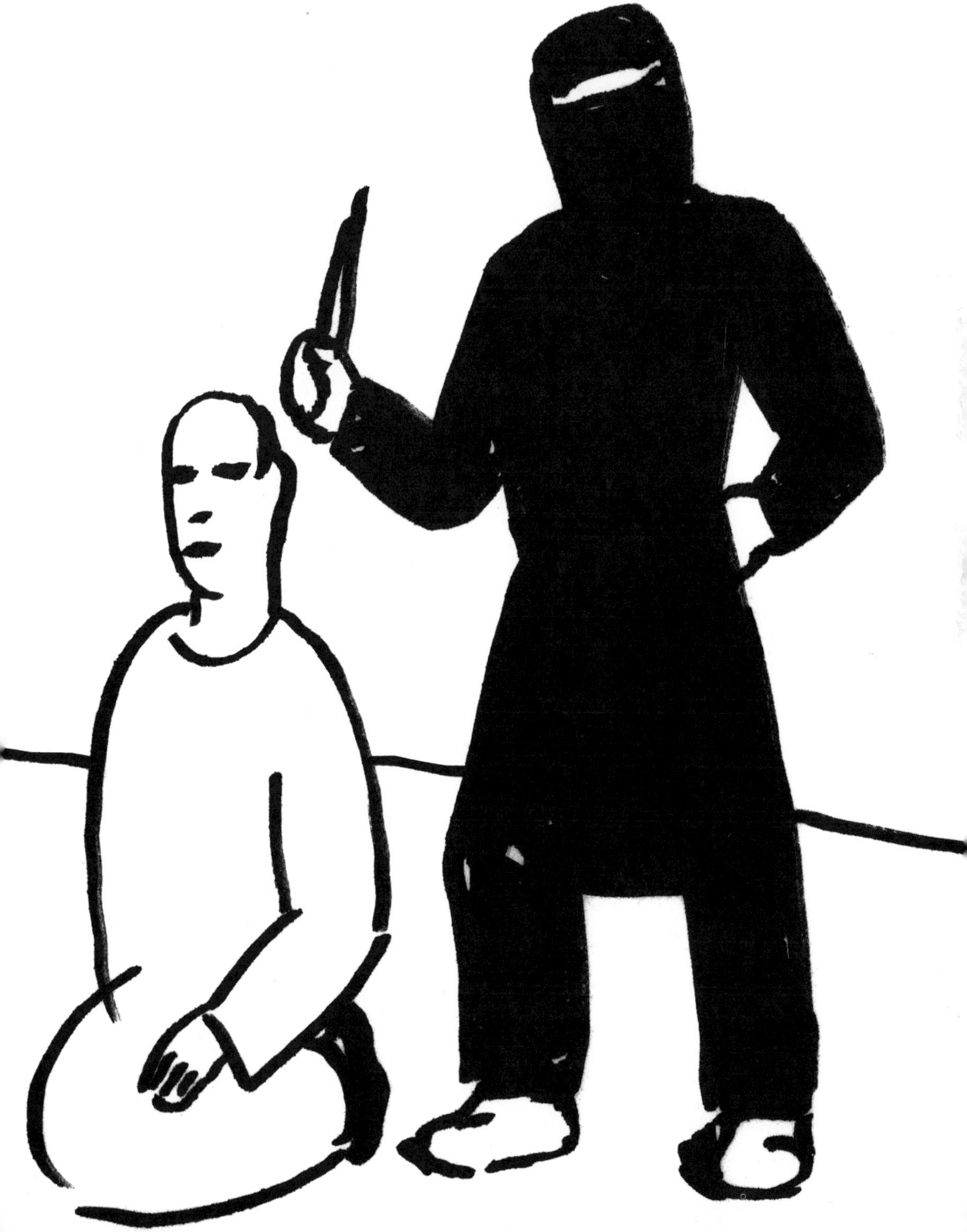

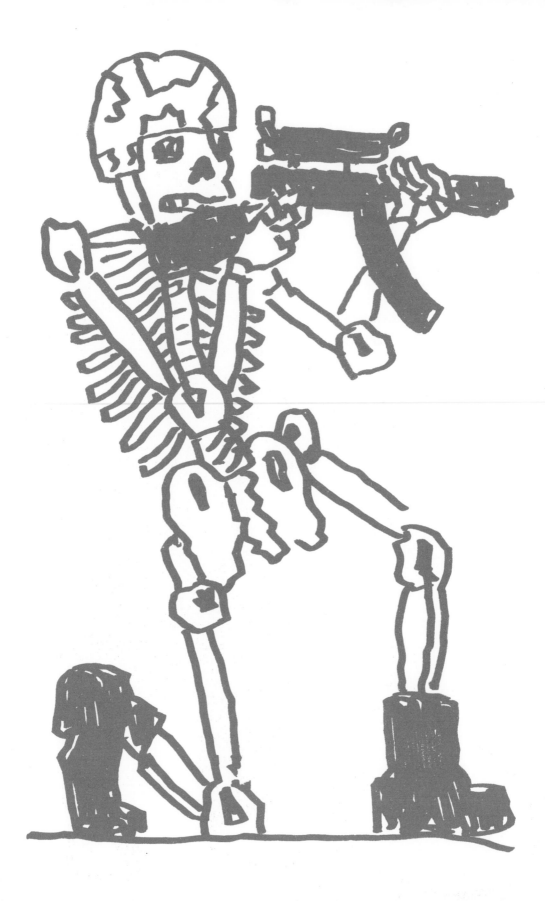

If we do not learn
from history we shall
be compelled to relive
it. True. But if we do not
change the future,
we shall be compelled
to endure it. And that
would be worse.

Alvin Toffler